P9-AGU-790

SECRET
GENEVA

Christian Vellas

Jonglez

We immensely enjoyed writing the *Secret Geneva* guide
and hope that, like us, you will continue to discover
the unusual, secret and lesser-known facets of this city.
Accompanying the description of some sites, you will
find historical information and anecdotes that will let you
understand the city in all its complexity.
Secret Geneva also sheds light on the numerous yet
overlooked details of places we pass by every day.
These details are an invitation to pay more attention
to the urban landscape and, more generally, to regard
our city with the same curiosity and attention we often
feel when travelling…

Comments on this guide and its contents, as well as
information on sites not mentioned, are welcome
and will help us to enrich future editions.

Don't hesitate to contact us:
• Jonglez Publishing,
  17, boulevard du Roi,
  78000 Versailles, France
• E-mail: info@jonglezpublishing.com

CONTENTS

LOWER CITY

CONTENTS

CANTON

INDEX

CONTENTS

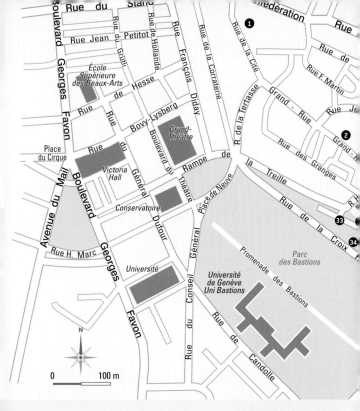

OLD CITY

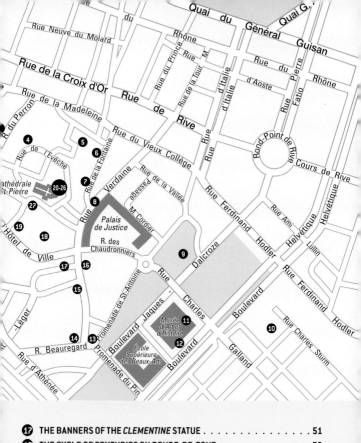

THE LAST PILLAR OF THE FORMER DOMES

5, rue de la Cité
• Trams 12, 16, 17, Bel-Air/Cité stop

> *A typical Genevan solution to housing crises*

A t the end of rue de la Cité, a few metres before the Escalade fountain and the opening onto Rues-Basses, there is a tall wooden pillar supporting the corner of an upper floor.

This pillar is the last trace of the various solutions to the housing crises that plagued Geneva time and time again throughout its history.

Constrained within its walls, the city had no choice but to expand upwards when housing had to be found for the flows of newcomers. Geneva's solution was to build "domes" overhanging the street supported by tall wooden pillars. These large frame constructions were often linked by horizontal beams.

There were four types of dome, distinguishable according to their beam structure. The first mention of the domes dates back to 1284.

Over time, they sprouted up in Rues-Basses, Molard, Longemalle, Bourg-de-Four, place de la Fusterie, rue de la Cité, rue Saint-Léger, and, on the right bank, place Saint-Gervais and all along the right side of rue de Coutance.

During the Reformation, when waves of Protestant refugees again arrived from France, even more domes were built. As the poor lacked the means to flee, most of the refugees were rather well-off and ready to invest in real estate. At first extra floors were added, but as that was still inadequate, new domes were built.

At the end of the 18th century, Geneva had several hundred of these additions jutting out into its main thoroughfares. Under the domes, pedestrians were sheltered from bad weather. "These giant parasols keep the already polluted air inside the rooms from circulating, but at least they serve as umbrellas!" complained a Geneva resident in 1824.

In Rues-Basses, shopkeepers had also set up stalls that encroached on the road from both sides. The city was becoming crammed, what was meant to be temporary was becoming permanent, and inhabitants feared fires could break out.

The demolition of the domes started around 1825. Progressively, these ageing structures were torn down until, in 1854, only a dozen remained. The last dome, the one on place de la Fusterie, disappeared in 1875.

The Confédération Centre commercial group, on rue de la Confédération, wanted to revive the spirit of these old domes, even if this "spirit" is often ignored by passers-by, who fail to recognize such specialized architectural references.

ALBERT GALLATIN: A "GENEVAN" AMERICAN WHO HELPED THE U.S. BUY LOUISIANA FROM NAPOLEON

The United States owes a lot to rue des Granges! Albert Gallatin (1761-1849), a man who played a large role in the country's consolidation, was born at number 7. Orphaned at a very young age, he was raised by his grandmother, Louise-Suzanne Gallatin-Vaudenet, a friend of Voltaire. In 1780, at the age of 19, he secretly left Geneva to avoid being forced to join the troops of Frederick II of Hesse, as his family wished, and embarked for the United States, which had declared its independence four years earlier. Lumberjack, trapper, French professor at Harvard, then pioneer (at 25, he received his inheritance and bought a large property in Pennsylvania), he led the dynamic life of a colonist.

Having received his American citizenship in 1785, Albert Gallatin founded the small colony of New Geneva along with other Genevan immigrants in 1789. It became the home of "A. Gallatin & Company", an industrial and agricultural company. It was during this period that his political career began. Indeed, a year earlier, Albert Gallatin had participated in the "Anti-Federalist" movement, which would later become the Republican Party.

He quickly ascended the political ranks. As a member of the Republican Party, he narrowly lost the Senate race in 1793 -- he could not be elected because he had not been an American citizen long enough (he was just one year short). U.S. Secretary of the Treasury from 1801 to 1813, it was notably thanks to him that the country was able to negotiate an $11 million loan to buy Louisiana from Napoleon.

In 1815, Gallatin, accompanied by his son James, took advantage of a trip to Europe to visit his hometown. He spent a month in Geneva and stayed on rue de la Cité, at the home of a relative, Madame Naville-Gallatin.

The glory of this "Genevan" American was such that, at his death, one of Missouri's three tributaries was named after him. The other two were named after Jefferson and Madison, the U.S. presidents with whom he worked.

7, rue des Granges
Bus 3, Place Neuve stop
Bus 36, Hôtel-de-Ville stop

CAMILLO CAVOUR, THE FATHER OF ITALIAN UNIFICATION, LIVED IN GENEVA

Considered the main architect of Italy's unification, Camillo Cavour spent part of his youth at the home of his maternal grandparents, the Boissier-Sellon family, at number 2 rue des Granges. Cavour (1810-1861) also regularly spent time at the castle owned by his cousin, Count Eugène de Roussy de Sales, at Thorens, in the nearby region of Savoy.

It was while he was prime minister of the kingdom of Piedmont-Sardinia that Cavour cleverly manoeuvred to successfully unify the majority of the country under the Italian crown (his secret negotiations with Napoleon III were a decisive factor). When he died of malaria in June 1861, only Venice and Rome had yet to become part of unified Italy.

Camillo Cavour defended state-organized lotteries with some cynicism, arguing that they constituted an additional tax for imbeciles. Indeed, in the 18th and 19th centuries, the Genevan authorities, like other European countries, had the habit of organizing lotteries to help the General Hospital or finance city projects.

The splendid edifice on rue des Granges, listed as a historic monument in 1923, was finally bought by the City of Geneva in 1955. To furnish the spacious rooms, the authorities accepted the offer of Countess Zoubov, who owned a remarkable collection of 18th-century *objets d'art*, in 1959. They agreed on an exchange: Geneva could welcome its official guests in a prestigious setting, while the countess was allowed to live in the other private rooms of this beautiful residence. Of Argentinean origins (she had wed a Russian nobleman in 1922 at Cologny), she dedicated the

site to the memory of her daughter Tatiana, who had died in a road accident in Uruguay at the age of 18, as a plaque above the entrance indicates.

The Zoubov collection comprises rare pieces of furniture marked with the trademarks of prestigious French craftsmen, ceramics, Sèvres porcelain, precious carpets, and paintings by such artists as Vigée-Lebrun.

2, rue des Granges
Bus 3, Place Neuve stop
Bus 36, Hôtel-de-Ville stop

THE DOOR OF THE PICTET HOUSE

15, Grand-Rue
• Bus 36, Hôtel-de-Ville stop

A true marvel

One of Grand-Rue's jewels, the Pictet House, was built in three years (1690-1693) for mayor Jacques Pictet. In fact, in today's terms, it was more like "heavy" renovation work that master builder Abraham Calame carried out, as Pictet had bought four houses to transform them into one. The party walls were kept and a new façade was built to unify the structure, along with, in the courtyard, a remarkable stairwell tower to replace the four flights of steps that used to face the street.

The details are sumptuous: casement windows connected by string courses and panels, sculpted decorations, and exceptional ironwork.

The most spectacular element, however, is the front door, fully open to the gaze of passers-by, in contrast to the house itself which is closed to the public. The door's pilasters support a splendid entablature, a layout that pleasantly breaks up the uniformity of the façade. The doorframe is a woodworking masterpiece, a prime example of what late-17th-century Genevan woodworkers were able to accomplish.

This marvel was restored in 1946-1947.

"ONE OF THE CRUELLEST ABUSES OF THE LUXURY THAT DEVOURED US FOR SO LONG..."

In order to reconcile the taste for these sumptuous dwellings with the Genevan austerity inherited from Calvinist edicts, severe laws were enacted. Until 1747, for example, it was forbidden to hang more than one mirror in a room. The size of the mirror allowed depended on your social class. The well-to-do knew how to get around these regulations, however.

In 1794, a century after the Pictet House was built, the Genevan revolutionaries proclaimed: "One of the cruellest abuses of the luxury that devoured us for so long was the obsession of the rich to display their uselessness in vast apartments."

THE LAST "FIRE-POT" IN GENEVA

③

Rue du Perron
• Tram 12, Molard stop
• Bus 36, Hôtel-de-ville stop

*A vestige
of the former
lighting system*

At the top of rue du Perron, behind the fountain, a curious rusted iron structure is attached to the wall. This is the last vestige of the former pitch lighting system that served Geneva for almost three centuries. Every night, this "fire-pot" was filled with a mix of resin and tar that was set on fire to light the intersection. Calvin thus enjoyed its invaluable glow when heading home from the cathedral.

Public lighting was a constant concern for Genevan authorities because of the insecurity that reigned over the city after nightfall. However, it was not until 1526 that a decision regarding the installation of these structures at main intersections can be found in the Council's archives. These "fire-pots" were only to be lit in "case of necessity", as the cost of the lighting was prohibitive.

In 1654, the chosen method was to ask residents to place candles in their windows to guide firemen during fires or alarms. This measure was optional at first, but soon became obligatory for those living on lower floors.

Generally, however, Geneva remained in the dark. Not until the arrival of foreign troops in 1782 (they came to restore the government of the aristocrats, which had become overrun by the bourgeoisie) was a modicum of public lighting installed.

The Marquis of Jaucourt, commander of this coalition, ordered the multiplication and regular lighting of the "fire-pots".

During the Genevan Revolution (1794), the councillors gave up this luxury. They started by eliminating 108 streetlights and classifying the others into three categories: the "indispensible", the "necessary", and the "useful until 10pm". During the French occupation, all streetlights were extinguished twice – in May 1799 and December 1800 – because the city's coffers were empty. After thirteen months of darkness, 84 lanterns were relit, including eight that were left burning all night.

Progress finally arrived in foreign cities, although belatedly, thanks to the "smokeless oil lamp", invented by Geneva resident Aimé Argand in 1784. Quinquet, a Parisian, stole Argand's idea, and, in the end, it was lamps perfected by N. Paul that lit Geneva's streets under mayor Frédéric-Guillaume Maurice's administration (1801-1814).

THE "SECRET" MONETIER PASSAGE ❹

Rue du Perron
- Tram 12, Molard stop
- Bus 36, Hôtel-de-ville stop

*A narrow
alley open
one day a year*

On the day celebrating the Escalade, the Sunday evening nearest 11 December, you should take advantage of the only opportunity to discover the Monetier passage. The rest of the year, it is closed by a gate.

This alley, which leads from the middle of rue du Perron to the bottom of rue des Barrières, is particularly narrow. Corpulent visitors risk getting stuck, and even slim ones must turn sideways at times to get through.

At the Perron-side entrance, a rough map of the neighbourhood, engraved in the wall, indicates the location of Saint Peter's Cathedral and the Magdalene Church, along with the inscription: "Monetier Passage, at the foot of the enclosure of Saint Peter's capitular cloister, 12th-13th C".

This passage is a vestige of a pathway that led under the walls at the end of the 5th century, during the Late Roman Empire. The most commonly accepted route for this first wall is the following: rue de l'Hôtel-de-Ville, beneath the Auditory choir, down rue de la Fontaine, the Muret passage, the Monetier passage, rue de la tour de Boël at the top of impasse Bémont, then the slopes of Tertasse and Treille hills, the Baudet Tower and the corner of the former rue du Manège (now rue René-Louis Piachaud).

The Monetier passage was one of the many more-or-less secret paths that allowed the defenders of the Bourgeois Militia to pass through inner courtyards and connected alleyways in order to reach their combat positions quickly. The various sections were each closed off by doors. To reach rue de la Fontaine from here, you took the Muret passage (see page 29).

Over time, the Monetier passage survived, as succeeding owners never wanted to build directly up to their neighbours' home (party walls were sources of dispute). These narrow alleys between the buildings thus served for rain and sewer drainage.

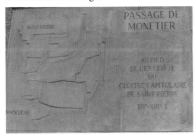

THE TWISTS AND TURNS OF RUE DES BARRIÈRES

5

• Bus 36, Tram 12, Molard stop

> *The remains of a military defence system*

I t is dark, cold and slippery. At night, it is a dangerous back-alley. Consisting of flights of steps, sloping ramps, side landings and clever turns, rue des Barrières is a perfect example of the art of deflection, invented by soldiers to fight off assailants. Indeed, the proliferation of blind angles kept the enemy from firing arrows or bullets while allowing the defenders to easily aim at their targets. It is a feature of the science of fortifications in its most twisted form.

The remains of walls 2 metres thick found in the cellars of the buildings lining the street, and notably three narrow openings (old embrasures?) overlooking rue des Barrières, suggest that this was an advance defence post protecting the bishopric on the lakeside. The level of Lake Geneva (Lac Léman) used to be much higher and closer to the upper part of the town.

In the past, the upper end of rue des Barrières was closed off by the Cloister gate and was thus the most direct route taken by the monks when they went to feast in the lower part of town. At the time, one of the oldest inns in Geneva, *La Mule*, was located at the bottom of this street.

THE SCULPTED BOMB BEHIND MAGDALENE ❻ CHURCH

Rue Toutes-Âmes, rue de la Fontaine
• Trams 12, 16, 17, Molard stop

A bomb shelter under the Old City

O n the small esplanade between rue Toutes-Âmes and the bottom of rue de la Fontaine, one of the three doors set into the hillside is decorated with an unsettling agraffe (a decorative carving on the keystone). It shows an enormous bomb falling between Rousseau Island, recognizable by its poplar trees, and the towers of Saint Peter's Cathedral.

These discreet doors hide the entrance to a bomb shelter that is perfectly concealed in the heart of the Old City.

In 1939, several shelters were built to protect Geneva's citizens from bombings. Although it was a neutral country, Switzerland risked being the victim of the error of pilots flying to or from attacks on enemy targets. For this reason, a two-level shelter large enough to hold 1,200 people was built beneath Agrippa-d'Aubigné terrace, behind Magdalene Church.

WHEN GENEVA WAS MISTAKEN FOR GENOA

On the night of 11 June 1940, in three successive waves, English Armstrong-Whitworth A.W.38 Whitley planes from the Bomber Command flew over Geneva and released eight bombs over Champel, Plainpalais and Carouge (1h50). They fell on chemin Venel, chemin de la Roseraie, chemin des Croisettes, rue de la Ferme, rue Beau-Séjour and rue des Allobroges. Four people were killed and several dozen injured. What was the cause of this error? The pilots, who were flying at night and in busy skies, supposedly got off-position, mistaking Geneva for Genoa. The British government apologized and paid 1.2 million francs in compensation, a sum which also compensated for other damage caused by bombs dropped over Renens and Daillens in the canton of Vaud.

THE REMAINS OF MURET PASSAGE

❼

Between rue des Barrières and rue de la Fontaine
• Bus 36, Bourg-de-Four stop

The Monetier passage used to continue to the Muret (or Mouret) passage in the direction of rue de la Fontaine (formerly rue du Boule). Traces still remain, notably on Agrippa-d'Aubigné terrace, where a now walled-up gallery runs alongside the outer wall of the bishopric's former prison.

If you are curious enough to look through the narrow gate halfway down the passage, you will see a few steps cut into the slope. This short gallery leads to a rusted iron gate. It then plunges down a very steep flight of steps to rue de la Fontaine, where the walled-up entryway lies under thick ivy (photo opposite).

It is striking to compare the site as it is today with the way it was prior to

> *A passage through which Geneva's last bishop fled in 1533*

1924 (photo shown here). A three-storey building stood over the Muret passage.

The bishopric's prison had occupied the entire back section of this property since 1842, when it replaced the former bishops' residences. The prison was closed in 1914 and finally demolished in 1940.

Before 1842, the Muret passage was uncovered. According to legend, the last bishop of Geneva, Pierre de la Baume, supposedly fled through this passage by night in 1533.

THE STRANGE DESTINY
OF THE LUTHERAN CHURCH

8

20, rue Verdaine
• Tel.: 022 310 41 87
• http://www.luther-genf.ch/
• Tram 12 or 16. Bus 2, 6, 7, 9, 20, Molard stop
• Bus 36, Bourg-de-Four stop

An unlikely-looking church

In a curious fashion, the Lutheran Church of Geneva looks like anything but a church, the consequence of a convention signed in 1760 between its builders and the Republic of Geneva.

The reason for this uncommon agreement was the never-resolved opposition between the Calvinist and Lutheran dogmas. Martin Luther, a German priest in revolt against Rome, had posted ninety-five Reformist theses on the door of the church of Wittenberg twenty years before Calvin arrived in Geneva.

In Geneva, Lutherans were tolerated; they were not loved, but they were not hated either. The Calvinists treated them as straying brothers, divided by a few fundamental beliefs. For some things, like taking in refugees and helping the needy, they nevertheless shared the work, which led to the following agreement: in exchange for the right to build a private temple, provided that it did not look like a religious edifice on the outside, the Lutherans of Geneva would be responsible for providing aid not only to the poor of their parish, but

also to those of all the other non-Calvinist churches. The compromise suited the Lutheran Church, which was thus able to discreetly take care of its flock of primarily Nordic origins.

When the building was completed in 1766, it was the first non-Calvinist church in the reformed capital, but its followers were called to service by the cathedral bells. German has always been the church's primary language.

The castle of Allinges-Coudrée, a massive structure with crenellated walls and four corner towers, stood on the current site of the Lutheran church until 1665. In the 18th century, only one tower remained.

THE FORGOTTEN ORIGIN OF THE VALLETTE-MONNIER FOUNTAIN

9

Promenade Saint-Antoine
• Bus 36, Saint-Antoine stop

> *A fountain commemorating an exceptional friendship*

Two writers who were contemporaries, living in the same city, showing no jealousy, but instead mutual respect and love – rather rare! Philippe Monnier, born in 1864, was nevertheless quite different from Gaspard Vallette, born a few months later in 1865. Everything seemed to set them apart: their physical appearance, their convictions, their temperaments. Monnier was a man of imagination, dreams, and poetic enthusiasm. Vallette was a man of critical thought and rigour, qualities that led him to become editor-in-chief of *La Suisse* (1898-1903). Both of them died young (1911), but Monnier was first at the age of 47. Vallette, whose heart gave out at the age of 46, only outlived him by two weeks. "Vallette died because Monnier died," people said at the time. People talked of their exemplary complicity, like that of Montaigne and La Boétie. However, one of their contemporaries sketched a slightly different image of them: "You had to see them during their heated discussions, Monnier crazily riding off on his grand ideas and utopias, with Vallette brusquely unseating him, throwing him down to the ground of hard reality, using precise and mocking words – a very level-headed Don Quixote and a Sancho Panza enamoured of beauty and moral distinction." On the initiative of the students of Collège Calvin, a public fund was started to erect a monumental fountain in their memory. A true monument to friendship, medallions of the two writers, along with a list of their main works, are carved into one side of the fountain while, on the other side there are allegorical figures representing friendship and the inscription "*Amicitia Memor*".

Inaugurated on 20 April 1914, the Vallette-Monnier Fountain was designed by the Genevan sculptor Carl Albert Angst (1875-1965). The artist rests in the Cimetière des Rois (Cemetery of the Kings) at Plainpalais, under one of his sculptures entitled *Vers l'infini* (Towards Infinity).

THE BUST OF RODOLPHE TŒPFFER

Rue François-Lefort and rue Rodolphe-T pffer
• Bus 36, Eglise russe stop

I n a tiny square on rue François-Lefort stands the bust of Rodolphe Tœpffer, the work of his son, Charles. The son of the Genevan painter Adam Tœpffer, Rodolphe also wanted to become a painter, but, stricken by an eye disease at the age of 17, he was obliged to become a teacher instead. Towards the end of his life, he lost his sight entirely, passing away at the age of 47, in 1846. Not far from here, at number 14 Promenade Saint-Antoine, stood the boarding school where he applied his progressive methods. He often took his students on long "school trips" lasting a couple of weeks, during which their academic knowledge was confronted with the reality of the regions they visited.

> **The inventor of comic strips was Genevan!**

Rodolphe Tœpffer then recounted these travels in funny stories illustrated

with sketches. Notably encouraged by Goethe, who was enchanted by the inventiveness and novelty of the approach, Tœpffer began creating albums that became the origin of comic strips. There was Monsieur Jabot, Monsieur Crépin, Monsieur Cryptogame, and Monsieur Vieux-Bois to name a few... veritable masterpieces of sparkling wit.

TŒPFFER: SOURCE OF INSPIRATION FOR GUSTAVE DORÉ, PICASSO

Tœpffer's drawings influenced many great artists, who were not ashamed to admit how much they owed him. Notable among them were Gustave Doré and Picasso, who, in his youth, had comic strips published in American newspapers.

THE MYSTERIOUS LADIES OF THE TROINEX STONE

❶

Musée d'Art et d'Histoire
2, rue Charles-Galland
• Bus 36, Saint-Antoine stop

One of Geneva's enigmas

The Museum of Art and History's Ladies Stone is an erratic boulder on which four female figures have been engraved. A remnant of an ancient site of worship, it has exhausted generations of researchers who have only revealed part of its secrets.

It is believed that the stone was first used near the end of the Neolithic period and up to Roman times, when it was carved. In the beginning, there were several blocks at the site, which were apparently converted into a tumulus during the Bronze Age. The site was rediscovered in 1819 by Frenchman Eusèbe Salverte. The tumulus, located in the village of Troinex, was dominated by the Ladies Stone, which was transported to Parc des Bastions in 1872. Then, in 1877, the tumulus was razed to the ground to realign a road.

The most troubling discovery was that of four tombs. Three of them contained two skeletons each lying head to foot, while the fourth held just one skeleton. The disposition of the remains inspired several legends, one of which claimed a powerful lord repudiated each of his consecutive wives and had them buried here, the body of the fourth tomb being that of the lord himself.

Another surprise was the discovery of the shattered skulls (and only the skulls) of two men and two women at the base of the tumulus. Are these remains, which roughly date from 800 BC, the result of human sacrifice?

The Ladies Stone is on show in the interior courtyard of the Museum of Art and History. Troinex recovered two other menhirs from the site and placed them in front of the town hall in 1999, along with a plastic, but faithful, imitation of the Ladies Stone.

STELE TO THE GLORY OF THE GOD MITHRA ⑫

Musée d'Art et d'Histoire
2, rue Charles-Galland
• Bus 36, Saint-Antoine stop

In 201, the legionnaire Firmidius gave thanks to Mithra

Thanks to a Roman legionnaire, the existence of a cult dedicated to the god Mithra beneath the current site of Saint Peter's Cathedral was confirmed. In 1752, a stone engraved with a Latin inscription was discovered in the cathedral basement. The inscription can be translated as follows: *To the invincible god, to the spirit of this place. Firmidius Severinus, soldier of the Eighth Augustan Legion, pious, faithful, constant, resilient, after twenty-six years of service, dedicated this altar freely and justly following a prayer for his salvation. Erected during the consulship of Mucianus and Fabianus.* This "invincible god" is none other than Mithra, whose worship spread throughout the Empire and was particularly followed by the military. The "spirit of the place" is believed to be another local divinity (but historians remain divided on the question).

The Eighth Augustan Legion of our retiring legionnaire was in charge of defending the Rhine and was stationed in Strasbourg, where an important mithraeum was unearthed in 1911. The fidelity of this legion to Emperor Commodus during the revolt of 185 earned this unit the titles of *pia, fidelis, constans, commode*, the terms found on the altar discovered in

Geneva. The military service of legionnaires generally lasted twenty years, but the soldier Firmidius probably prolonged his service because of the turmoil in 193-197 that marked the beginning of Septimius Severus' reign. A detachment of the Eighth Legion was dispatched to Lyon, which undoubtedly explains why the veteran Firmidius decided to retire to Geneva. The altar to Mithra, dating from 201, was placed on Promenade des Bastions for a time (1888-1912). Today, it stands in the Museum of Art and History.

WHEN A BANKER BOUGHT "HIS" STREET...

Charles Galland, a senior "stockbroker", wanted a street to be named after him on his death. He lived on rue Tœpffer and could not properly think of taking the place of the illustrious illustrator. Yet nearby was rue de l'Observatoire (the street of the observatory created in 1722 by the astronomer Mallet) – perhaps a substitution was conceivable...

Galland, who died in 1901 at the age of 85, thus made a deal with the city authorities. He would bequeath 9 million gold francs to the city, which it could use as it saw fit, and, in return, a street would be named after him at this spot.

Such a gift could not be refused, so the street signs were changed after a rapid deliberation of the City Council. Galland's money was used for several constructions, including 3 million for the Museum of Art and History, which was built along his street. The project, which lasted from 1903 to 1910, was entrusted to architect Marc Camoletti. It is an imposing building, with columns, statues and busts scattered along the façade, as well as a double flight of steps. Jean Nouvel's project to enlarge the building, adopted in 2009, will provoke a clash of styles and periods over the next few years. If the project is not challenged, that is ...

And what about the observatory? Well, in 1967, its dome and telescopes were moved to Sauverny, on the border between Geneva and the Vaud region. In its place today stands a monumental sculpture by Henry Moore – *Reclining Figure: Arch Leg*. At the first hint of sunshine, the lawn around the statue is dotted with students from the nearby Collège Calvin.

MITHRAISM – A FASCINATING ANCIENT RELIGION FOR THE INITIATED

Mithraism is a religious cult centred around Mithra, a god of Iranian origin. Born from a rock, Mithra entered the world naked, bearing a knife and a torch and wearing a Phrygian cap. After having vanquished the Sun, he signed a pact with his former enemy and took his radiant crown, which became his attribute. Tirelessly hunting down evil, Mithra, aided by his dog, captured a bull, the symbol of the impetuous, animal forces one has to learn to master, and killed it. The bull's marrow miraculously gave birth to wheat, and from his blood sprang grapevines, as if death is necessary for life to begin... Ahriman, the god of evil, did not admit defeat, however. He sent a scorpion and a snake, but in vain. Mithra and the Sun celebrated their victory with an *agape* (feast), a word that is still used in some languages.

The worship of Mithra mainly took place in cellars and caves, not for reasons related to the darkness, as some critics have claimed, but rather because caverns symbolized the cosmos that participants tried to reach during the ceremonies.

Mithra was flanked by two torchbearers, Cautes and Cautopates, with whom he formed a triad (or Trinity). The former bore a lit torch representing the day, while the latter bore an extinguished torch directed towards the ground, symbolizing the night. These two figures, visually and otherwise, were simply representations of the same Mithra.

The concept of the voyage of the soul through the cosmos is central. One advanced on this path in 7 stages, related to the 7 planets, the 7 days of the week, 7 metals, and the 7 moods of the soul from which

one had to separate oneself progressively. Worship was clearly a way to advance on this path and to progressively free oneself from passions. The banquet, or *agape*, based on bread and wine, obviously recalls the Eucharist, and the sacrificing of the bull from which life was born strangely recalls the Crucifixion and Resurrection.

Spread through the West from the 1st century BC, Mithraism reached its height in the 3rd century AD, before being replaced by Christianity.

CHRISTMAS OWES ITS DATE OF 25 DECEMBER TO THE WINTER SOLSTICE AND MITHRAISM...

Contrary to popular belief, no Christian text says that Jesus was born on the night of 24 December. In 354, Pope Liberious set 25 December as the official date of Christmas in an attempt to fight the pagan Roman religions, and especially Mithraism, which celebrated the birth of its god Mithra on 25 December, the date of the winter solstice (the winter solstice was not celebrated on a specific day and did not always fall on 21 December, at least not until the reform of the Gregorian calendar – which, by the way, was one of the reasons the calendar was created).

The Church's takeover of this date also led to the creation of a beautiful symbolism. At the time of year when the days are the shortest and the night rules supreme, the birth of Christ was a formidable symbol of the day rising again and of light shining at last, chasing away the darkness and announcing the Resurrection.

Before this date, Christians celebrated the birth of Christ on 6 January, the same day as the Adoration of the Magi. Only the Armenian Apostolic Church still celebrates Christmas on this date. The Orthodox churches that celebrate Christmas on a date other than 25 December actually do so on the same day (25 December) but according to the Julian calendar, which shifts the date.

Note also that, according to tradition, Jesus was not born in the year 0, but rather in −5 or −7...

FRANZ LISZT AND MARIE D'AGOULT'S HOUSE OF LOVE

13

Place Franz-Liszt
• Bus 36, Franz-Liszt stop

Remembering a scandalous couple

On the façade of this beautiful corner building, a pink marble plaque bears the composer's profile and the following inscription: "Hungarian master Franz Liszt stayed in this house from 1835 to 1836". The time spent with Marie d'Agoult, his lover at the time, was brief but long enough to have a plaque put up and the square named after the pianist. Countess Marie d'Agoult had abandoned her husband and children, as well as her spectacular Parisian lifestyle, to run off with the handsome Franz. She was 29, and the pianist (a former seminarian) was 23. They arrived in Geneva and settled in the house at the intersection of rues Tabazan, Beauregard and Étienne-Dumont, at the end of Promenade Saint-Antoine. This scandalous couple were snubbed by high society. One of the rare Genevans to welcome them was the young James Fazy, who even went so far as to sign false declarations at the registry office when the two lovers had their first child, Blandine, in 1835. Marie d'Agoult prided herself on her writing, but at the time a woman had to sign under a male name if she wished to find a publisher. She did not write sentimental novels, however. Under the pseudonym Daniel Stern, she wrote a very serious work, *History of the Revolution of 1848*. Her friend, George Sand, had to bend to the same reality, she who bore the promising name of Aurore (Dawn)... George Sand joined the couple in Geneva. Franz Liszt only gave a few lessons at the Conservatory, so they were not living in the lap of luxury. A suitor had to be found for George Sand, who shocked Genevan society by dressing as a man and smoking cigars in public. It was major Pictet, the son of the illustrious Charles Pictet de Rochemont, who stepped forward, but he was not rewarded for the effort. Following an excursion to the foot of Mont-Blanc, the novelist ferociously mocked him in her *Dixième lettre d'un voyageur* (Tenth Letter of a Traveller). After leaving Geneva, Marie d'Agoult and Liszt's love affair cooled and finally ended. Their liaison officially ended in 1846.

Liszt and the countess had three children, including Cosima, who returned to Geneva twenty-nine years later. After a first marriage, she lived in Switzerland with Richard Wagner, whom she eventually married. When Wagner died, Cosima, an unrelenting heiress, vigilantly controlled the deceased composer's royalties. Raised in a musical family, she had heard it all before!

SINISTER TABAZAN'S SHOP SIGN

⑭

9, rue Tabazan
• Bus 36, Franz-Liszt stop

The address of Geneva's last executioner

The shop sign at number 9, rue Tabazan represents an executioner with his hood and large sword. His official uniform was black and purple. This is where François Tabazan (1534-1624), Geneva's last executioner, lived. The last of a long line of executioners (the sons of executioners were socially barred from any other profession), this ultimate specialist was an expert of strappado, knucklebones and the boot, as well as a master of the grand spectacle of the wheel located on place du Molard, and a virtuoso with an axe. He had his hour of glory the day after the Escalade of 1602, on the night of 11 December (Julian calendar).

After Duke Charles-Emmanuel's Savoyards had been pushed back vigorously, Tabazan had to hang thirteen – or fourteen? – illustrious prisoners before cutting off their heads. He then beheaded fifty-four assailants who had died in the combat. Their skulls were then fixed on pikes and left for all to see for six months.

It was customary for the executioner to collect the clothes of his torture victims and resell them, so one man's misery was another man's wealth. The remuneration for a decapitation was rather modest: ten florins (or a few hundred Swiss francs), and the work was irregular.

The Tabazan family became part of the Genevan bourgeoisie in 1490. They were thus true Genevans, even if the plaque displayed in the street states that the executioner's ancestors were Savoyards from Chilly.

RUE CHAUSSE-COQ: A REMINDER OF THE BROTHELS OF YESTERYEAR

• Bus 36, Franz-Liszt stop

I n the past, the brothel quarter was located two steps from the cathedral. The names of the main streets were explicit: rue des Belles-Filles (beautiful girls), rue Chausse-Con (fit bitch), cul-de-sac du Vieux-Bordel (old brothel). As these streets had lost their original vocation (already in Roman times, one of them was named *Carreria Lupanaris*), the new inhabitants were ashamed of their address, especially given the number of clergymen who lived in the area.

Beautiful girls "fit" for young cocks

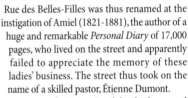

Rue des Belles-Filles was thus renamed at the instigation of Amiel (1821-1881), the author of a huge and remarkable *Personal Diary* of 17,000 pages, who lived on the street and apparently failed to appreciate the memory of these ladies' business. The street thus took on the name of a skilled pastor, Étienne Dumont.

Impasse du Vieux-Bordel, which opened onto Promenade Saint-Antoine, became rue Maurice, after a clever mayor (he had to keep both parties happy) who held office during the French occupation (1801-1814).

Only rue Chausse-Con was left. It was hypocritically renamed rue Chausse-Coq (fit cock). The origin of this rather ribald name was the source of some debate. According to some historians, the "cocks" (young libertines, as they were called in the Middle Ages) were "fitted" at a good price at the shops of neighbourhood shoemakers and then led the good life in the nearby brothels.

At the time, these places of pleasure were perfectly regulated. The Council appointed the "queen of the harem", the madam in charge of keeping everything under control. This "social" structure disappeared around 1535.

In 1998, several municipal councillors attempted to give these streets back their former names. They were notably nostalgic for "Belles-Filles" and wanted to get rid of the severe "Étienne-Dumont". A motion was bitterly debated, but ultimately rejected.

GONDEBAUD
ROI DES BURGONDES
v. 480 – 516

PAR ROGER FERRIER
(1957)

THE STATUE OF GUNDOBAD AT BOURG-DE-FOUR

5-7, place du Bourg-de-Four
• Bus 36, Bourg-de-Four stop

Crouching in a niche on a wall of place du Bourg-de-Four, a polychrome statue of Gundobad, king of the Burgundians, shows a rather friendly bearded figure holding a sword between his legs. Don't be fooled: this monarch won the throne thanks to a succession of cleverly-planned family murders.

The Burgundian king in his niche

The sculptor who placed the statue here in 1957, Roger Ferrier, probably would have preferred his brother Godegisel, king of Geneva in 490, but Gundobad had him assassinated after setting the city on fire in 500. It was not his first crime. A few years before, Gundobad had had another of his brothers (Chilperic) killed, along with his wife and sons. He spared his brother's two daughters, Chroma and Clotilda, by adopting them since, as king's daughters, they could always be used as bargaining chips or to strengthen alliances.

The two sisters, who had adopted the Christian religion whereas the Burgundians were Arians, grew up in Geneva, in the castle built at Bourg-de-Four. Clovis, king of the Francs, who was also calculating how to neutralize the Burgundians and strengthen his ties to the Church, chose Clotilda to be his wife. Gundobad hesitated, but finally consented. The marriage, which was celebrated in Soissons in 493, was blessed by Bishop Remi.

It is regrettable that the beautiful and pious Clotilda has no statue of her own at Bourg-de-Four, as she certainly deserved one. Having converted Clovis, the Christianization of Western Europe occurred largely thanks to her, leading Pope Pelagius II to canonize her.

Clotilda and her sister Chroma had the Saint Victor Church built in Geneva. Constructed in the 5th century on the ruins of Roman ramparts, the Burgundian castle at Bourg-de-Four was also demolished. Over the centuries, its foundations served as a base for a long succession of fortresses and buildings, even up to the buildings present today.

THE BANNERS OF THE *CLEMENTINE* STATUE ⑰

Place du Bourg-de-Four
• Bus 36, Bourg-de-Four stop

The statue that denounces injustice

The work of sculptor Heinz Schwarz, the graceful statue on place du Bourg-de-Four bears proclamations, demands and denunciations all year long. Her long body thus unwittingly defends all causes.

Clementine, as she is officially named, is thus never entirely naked. She is habitually covered by banners, photocopied newspaper articles, and posters. Small candles are often left burning at her feet. She is clearly cosseted and watched over, and her ration of protests is constantly renewed. This anorexic child offers a bit of reading to passers-by, pushing them to revolt against all the injustices of the world in general, and of several districts of Geneva in particular. If the artist of this bronze statue had to do it over again, he would most certainly have shown her raising her fist.

So, where does Clementine's strange vocation come from? Placed here in 1974 by the City of Geneva's Contemporary Art Fund, the statue was primarily the melancholy companion of sparrows and pigeons for seven years. Her destiny changed on 24 February 1981.

On that day, Geneviève Piret, founder of the *Terre des femmes et Terre des enfants* (Land of women and land of children) association, passed by the statue with a heavy heart. She had just left the burial of Yolande, known as Yoyo, a regular of the Bourg-de-Four district and a prostitute. Broken by the obstacles that had kept her from changing her life, Yoyo had committed suicide. Geneviève Piret thus left a strong plea of protest on the statue, along with some flowers in memory of Yoyo. She had no idea that this gesture would henceforth be repeated, for other causes and demands, day after day and year after year, by herself and other anonymous protestors who need to express their daily revolts.

Of course, Genevans know the names of the people who feed Clementine's mild fits of anger. They can often be found in the columns of the *Tribune de Genève* (Geneva Tribune), in the letters to the editor, proclaiming the same indignations and spouting their anger.

THE CYCLE OF CENTURIES ON BOURG-DE-FOUR

(18)

Place du Bourg-de-Four
• Bus 36, Bourg-de-Four stop

> *Two castles for one square*

Six streets join at the heart of the Old City on place du Bourg-de-Four. There is some debate as to the origin of the square's name. Some believe it is an Allobroges term given long ago to this district built outside the city walls (Borg de Feur means "village outside"). For others, the name is a corruption of the Latin words *Forum des Burgondes*. What is certain is that this square was the site of the cattle market for many years.

Two castles bordered the square. That of the counts of Geneva was at the beginning of rue de l'Hôtel-de-Ville. It was destroyed in 1320, but one of its gates, which closed off the Old City, survived to 1840. It is here that, accompanied by his executioner, the lord of Gaillard Castle, the only person authorized for the function, would come to retrieve the prisoners condemned to death. An iron collar was erected on the square in 1548 and was used for nearly two centuries. At the beginning of rue de l'Hôtel-de-Ville, you can still see a section of the massive wall against which part of the castle used to stand. Its main gate would have been located at what is now number 14.

The other castle was that of Coudrée, which was progressively demolished up to the 18th century. It was located where the Lutheran Church now stands.

WHEN NUMBER 1, GRAND-RUE WAS NUMBER 237...

In 1782, Geneva, which had no house numbering system, was equipped with one. This new measure was the result of an order from the commander of the French troops that had arrived in July 1782 along with two other allied forces (Bern and Sardinia) to restore power to the Genevan aristocracy, which had been removed by the populace.

The numbers painted on the buildings – in black on a white background – followed a natural order along the contours of the different districts, from the periphery to the city centre. So, on the left bank, number 1, Grand-Rue was number 237. On the right bank, number 1 was located on place des XXII-Cantons, and number 252 was at the extreme southern point of the island. At first, the population had trouble accepting this change, and the numbers and street names were often removed. There were two reasons for this. On the one hand, it was a form of resistance to an initiative of the foreign forces, and, on the other hand, many inhabitants felt this numbering system was an intolerable intrusion into their privacy.

Not until 1860 was the current system adopted, using even and odd numbers on each street.

Place de la
Taconnerie

RUE DE LA TACONNERIE STREET SIGN ⑲

Corner of rue de l'Hôtel-de-Ville
• Bus 36, Taconnerie stop

> *Geneva's most photographed street sign?*

Rue de la Taconnerie makes many francophone tourists chuckle. Its street sign, under which people sometimes innocently have their mother-in-law pose for a photo, is one of the most photographed signs in Geneva.

To set things right, the word *taconnerie* is not at all a contraction of the words *ta* (your) and *connerie* (stupidity)!

The word *tacon* could simply refer to the leather used by shoemakers in the past. Another explanation would be a link to the honourable Tacon family which was well-known in the 6th and 7th centuries.

This short street that now leads to Saint Peter's Cathedral was once a dead end closed off by the grain exchange.

THE SITE OF THE TUMULTUOUS LOVE AFFAIR BETWEEN EUGÈNE SUE AND LUCIEN BONAPARTE'S GRANDDAUGHTER, 30 YEARS HIS JUNIOR

At number 6, rue de la Taconnerie stands a beautiful seven-storey residence that was the highest in Geneva for many years. This is where writer Eugène Sue, author of *Le Juif errant* (The Wandering Jew), lived. Exiled by Emperor Napoleon III, he found himself in the shoes of his famous hero, but had trouble accepting his fate. When he was 53, he had a tumultuous love affair with the Countess of Solms, 21-year-old Marie Wyss-

Bonaparte. The relationship ended badly. In 1857, the serial writer of *Mystères de Paris* (Mysteries of Paris) succumbed to food poisoning after having picnicked in the country at the invitation of James Fazy, a great Genevan politician.

The Countess of Solms, granddaughter of Lucien Bonaparte, ruined the life of her lovers. Nicknamed "Princess brouhaha", she was sent away from Paris by her imperial cousin. After the Genevan episode, she went to Italy where she seduced prime minister Urbano Ratazzi and got him to marry her in 1860. She very soon cheated on him with King Emmanuel II, whom she also terrorized with her excesses, whims, provocations and mischief.

WHO WAS JEAN DE BROGNY?

Noted for his intelligence, Jean de Brogny climbed all the rungs of the ecclesiastical ladder. Robert of Geneva, a Savoyard prelate who became the first antipope as Clement VII, asked Brogny to join him in Avignon, where he had chosen to set up. At 37, Brogny published a "Brevarium juris", which became the authoritative work on the subject. He quickly accumulated the highest offices before breaking with antipope Benedict XIII (el Papa Luna) in 1409 and leading the papal court of Avignon to the Council of Pisa to end the schism. Brogny presided over the Council of Constance (1414-1418) and was bishop of Geneva – although he did not live there – from 1423 to 1426.

THE BAS-RELIEF OF THE PIG KEEPER

Exterior corner of the Chapel of the Maccabees
Saint Peter's Cathedral
• Bus 36, Cathédrale stop

Did Cardinal Jean de Brogny raise pigs?

Did the future Cardinal Jean de Brogny raise pigs when he was an adolescent in his native village of Brogny, near Annecy? Legend affirms it and there is no lack of evidence seeming to confirm this fine story. One such piece of evidence is the sculpted figure at the corner of the exterior façade of the Chapel of the Maccabees, which was built in 1405 for the cardinal, who wished to be buried there. The sculpture represents a young, barefoot man wearing a cape who is sheltered under a tree along with two pigs. Another unsettling piece of evidence is located in the temple of Jussy, where there is a three-person stall that supposedly came from the Chapel of the Maccabees. On one side of the stall, a man with three pigs can be seen under an oak tree.

These explanations were criticized, however, in a 1924 study by Genevan historian Waldemar Deonna. Indeed, he illustrated that Jean de Brogny had never been a pig farmer or a peasant, as his family belonged to the Savoyard

gentry. The pig-keeping anecdote was probably invented in the mid-17th century and is similar to the one attributed to Pope Sixtus V, who also supposedly kept pigs during his youth. Similarly, the shoe story, in which a Genevan cobbler gives a pair of shoes to a young, penniless man who has just arrived in Geneva ("You can pay me for them when you're cardinal!"), was supposedly invented much later (around 1660), by the powerful Genevan cobbler's guild. Sixtus V is also said to have been the recipient of a shoemaker's generosity... that makes quite a lot of coincidences! The ultimate explanation actually lies in the fact that the pig keeper could symbolize the prodigal son of the New Testament, who is often shown watching pigs under a tree (see photo).

WHY IS THE CHAPEL CALLED THE CHAPEL OF THE MACCABEES?

The Chapel of the Maccabees gets its name from a donation given by Count Amadeus VIII of Savoy, the future antipope Felix V. When the chapel was built, the count donated relics that supposedly came from the Jewish family of Judas Maccabeus, who had chased the Greek priests of Solomon's Temple from Jerusalem in 167 BC.

THE ENIGMA OF "APOLLO'S HEAD"

Saint Peter's Cathedral
• Bus 36, Cathédrale stop

*A puzzling
chubby-cheeked
figure behind
the cathedral*

The tradition which claimed that Saint Peter's Cathedral had been built over an ancient temple dedicated to Apollo had never carried much weight. It was enough to start a legend, however.

About 15 metres up at the rear of the cathedral, near the Passage des Degrés-de-Poule, a round, chubby-cheeked sculpted figure can be seen. It was named "Apollo's head" despite the fact that it does not in the least resemble other known representations of this god. The belief that it could be Apollo undoubtedly came from the sculpture's round form, as the Greek god is linked to the Sun.

Numerous historians and archaeologists have studied this enigma, and some have suggested that the head was simply placed here to signal the dawn.

Others ultimately concluded that it was undoubtedly a sculptor's whim, of which there are so many examples in monuments from the Middle Ages. This hypothesis was reinforced when this part of the cathedral was repaired. When this unusual head was taken out together with the plaster holding it in place, the workers realized that it had not been sculpted into the new stone, but on the capital of a 12th-century column before being brought here when the Midi tower was built in the 13th century.

CLEMENT'S MARK BENEATH SAINT PETER'S

The cathedral's largest bell (and thus the one with the deepest sound), the current *Clémence* (Clement) was recast and hoisted back up to the steeple in 1902, thus taking the place of the two preceding Clements. The first was cast in 1407, but it cracked in 1866. It was replaced in 1867, but the bell cracked again in 1901.

In the past, for the sake of convenience, very large bells were cast directly at the church. So, when an archaeological dig beneath Saint Peter's revealed traces of the casting of the first Clement, there was much excitement.

The imprint left in the ground measured more than 2 metres in diameter and a mark in the shape of a six-pointed star could be seen where the wooden supports of the mould had stood.

This bell, named in homage to antipope Clement VII (Robert of Geneva), gave rhythm to the life of the city for centuries. The current Clement, which weighs 6,238 kilos, bears the following inscription: "Twice broken, I want to live again and always remind the children of the children of Geneva of old Clement's voice".

THE INSCRIPTION AGAINST THE "ROMAN ANTICHRIST"

Saint Peter's Cathedral
6, Cour Saint-Pierre and 2, rue de l'Hôtel-de-Ville
• Bus 36, Cathédrale stop and Hôtel-de-Ville stop

> **When d'Alembert was infuriated by an anti-Catholic engraving**

On the wall of the northern aisle of Saint Peter's Cathedral, a still-present Latin inscription is largely ignored by churchgoers. This inscription was nevertheless the source of a scandal at the time of Diderot and d'Alembert and it does nothing short of comparing the pope with the Antichrist!

The text may be translated as follows: "The tyranny of the Roman Antichrist having been struck down in the year 1535 and its superstitions abolished, the inviolable religion of Christ was re-established here in its purity and the church, through God's exceptional grace, was replaced in a better form. Simultaneously, as the city has defeated and chased away its enemies and thus regained its freedom thanks to a notable miracle, the council and people of Geneva have decided to have this inscription engraved and erected here, so that the memory may never die and serve as proof of their gratitude to God in the eyes of their descendants".

Engraved in 1558 on a bronze plaque and affixed to the façade of the

town hall, this inscription is also visible on a drawing by engraver Pierre Escuyer (1749-1834). Preserved when the walls were restored in the 17th century, this Latin text is a reminder that Geneva banned the Roman religion in 1535. In his *Essai sur les mœurs* (Essay on Morals), Voltaire summarized part of the inscription: "In memory of the grace God showed us for casting off the yoke of the Antichrist, abolishing superstition, and regaining our freedom".

In Diderot and d'Alembert's *Encyclopédie* are the following lines, signed by Alembert, under the article "Geneva" (1757): "Between the two doors of Geneva's city hall, one can still see a Latin inscription commemorating the abolition of the Catholic religion. In it, the pope is called the Antichrist; this expression, permitted by the fanaticism for liberty and novelty of a century that was still half-barbarian, today seems scarcely worthy of a city so imbued with the philosophic spirit. We venture to suggest that the Genevans replace this insulting and vulgar monument with an inscription that is truer, nobler and simpler. For Catholics, the pope is the head of the true Church, for reasonable and moderate Protestants he is a sovereign whom they respect as a prince without obeying him, but in a century such as ours, there is no one for whom he is still the Antichrist."

In 1814, as Geneva was preparing to enter the Swiss Confederation, which included Catholic cantons, it was clear that such an inscription could not remain on the front of an official building. It was removed and replaced by another bronze plaque of the same size (still there) bearing the names of the twenty-two citizens who had formed the provisional government and proclaimed the Republic of Geneva's return to independence on 31 December 1813.

The inscription denouncing the "Antichrist" was first transported to the sacristy of Saint Peter's Cathedral, then set into the cathedral, where it remains today.

SYMBOLS OF THE CATHEDRAL'S CAPITALS

Saint Peter's Cathedral
• Bus 36, Cathédrale stop

I t is a pity that the cathedral's capitals are so high. Visitors must thus admire their beauty and try to decipher their symbols from afar.

A veritable book in stone

The illegibility caused by the distance is worsened by the fact that their original colours have worn off. Only a few traces of vermilion allowed specialists to reconstitute the palette of the 15th-century polychromes, which were quite different from their current dull, uniform grey (one of the first of such attempts was suggested by J.-D. Blavignac in 1845).

To appreciate all the details of these forty-odd capitals, and to understand how the columns are numbered, the best source is one of the numerous specialized works on sale in the cathedral. Otherwise, you'll miss a great read...

One of the most stunning motifs, of the mermaid with a cleft tail, was carved on several capitals. It symbolizes the mythic image of the enticing woman, an image that is also reproduced on a misericord in Saint Gervais Temple.

Another rather common image is that of characters sticking out their tongues or spitting out acanthus leaves (acanthus symbolizes the glory of exceptional men, amongst whom are the architects who triumphed over the difficulties of their task).

There are also men with the bodies of animals (a symbol of man's conflict between his bestial urges and his possible spiritual elevation), birds with female heads (harpies were insatiable monsters who kidnapped children and supplied Hell with the souls of the dead. The Greek gods did not destroy them, because they used their wickedness to torment mortals). A series of animals, both real and mythical (griffons, dragons, harpies, chimeras) thus follow one after another atop the columns.

Of course, the Devil is also present. He is shown half-naked with a wide torso, horns and a double-pointed beard, riding a monster and looking straight ahead. Not far from him, angels strike down dragons and brandish crosses – Heaven is well-guarded. Indeed, Christ majestically reigns nearby, wearing his halo and with his right hand raised in benediction and his left resting on the Holy Book.

There are also several biblical scenes: Abraham about to sacrifice his son, Daniel in the lion's den, Salome dancing with her hands on her hips, and Herod holding a man's head by the hair, to name but a few.

THE ORPHEUS CAPITAL IN THE CATHEDRAL ❷④

Saint Peter's Cathedral
• Bus 36, Cathédrale stop

> *A curious pagan presence at Saint Peter's*

The presence of an image of Orpheus, a figure of pagan mythology, on one of the capitals of Saint Peter's Cathedral is rather troubling. Located on a half-pillar of a chapel, in one of the darkest corners of the cathedral (capital 35 IV-14, according to the official map), the capital is also marked with the name "ORPHEUS", engraved on the horned abacus. Curiously, such a precise indication is not given for the figures decorating most of the other capitals.

Orpheus is shown playing a viola da gamba while seated on a low chair, one leg crossed over his knee. Two eagles are perched on his shoulders. The sculptor has perfectly rendered the details of his clothing, the musical instrument, and the asymmetrical composition. Imagine the composition with the splendour of 15th-century polychromes, which made these sculptures vibrate with reds, blues, greens and golds.

In the 6th century BC, the myth of Orpheus gave rise to a religion founded on the belief in the immortality of the soul and in a cycle of reincarnations leading to an ultimate and definitive purification. This religion is sometimes considered to be one of the transitions between paganism and Christianity, as Orpheus was even venerated by the first Christians as a sort of prophet. Is it thanks to this interpretation that this monolith is found on the cathedral's capital?

THE MYTH OF ORPHEUS

Orpheus had received a lyre with seven strings, to which he added two more strings in remembrance of the nine Muses, the sisters of his mother, Calliope. He enchanted men and wild animals with his song, giving a soul to inanimate objects and delighting the gods. This gift turned out to be quite useful when he descended into Hell in search of his wife, Eurydice. Charmed, Cerberus and the Furies agreed to let the couple leave, but on one condition: Orpheus was forbidden to turn to look at Eurydice before having left the dark kingdom. Yet we know that Orpheus could not help himself... Having given up on women after this ordeal, he died torn apart by the maenads, the female followers of Dionysus, who were appalled by his indifference. His head, which was thrown into the Hebrus, floated to Lesbos. Zeus placed his lyre among the constellations at the request of Apollo and the Muses, who gathered poor Orpheus' remains and buried them at the foot of Olympus.

THE MISERICORDS
OF SAINT PETER'S CATHEDRAL

Saint Peter's Cathedral
• Bus 36, Cathédrale stop
• Summer hours (1 June to 30 September): 9:30am–6:30pm, Monday to Saturday, and 12pm–6:30pm on Sunday
• Winter hours (1 October to 31 May): 10am–5:30pm, Monday to Saturday, and 12pm–5:30pm on Sunday

Some often provocative sculptures

Saint Peter's has thirty-two misericords divided into two rows of eleven under the seats of the high and low stalls of the southern aisle, with ten others under the low stalls of the choir. Here, we concentrate on the most original, or most provocative, ones.

The first of the high stalls shows a squatting man defecating. This scatological theme is not rare in cathedrals and can often be found in other religious edifices in Europe and in 15th- and 16th-century engravings. Perhaps it was a desire to defy the established order?

Second misericord: a dog eating sausages. This subject, found in the row of low stalls in the form of a dog chewing on a bone, supposedly represents envy, one of the seven deadly sins.

Eighth misericord: the tortoise often represents greed – as does the snail – and is also considered to be a lean meat that Catholics could eat on Friday.

Eleventh misericord: a man bent over hides his head in a large hood, a symbol illustrating a person who refuses to see?

First misericord of the low stalls: a grimacing man wearing a tight cap. This distorted face could illustrate lunacy. This was a popular theme, linked to manifestations of the Devil.

Ninth misericord: a crayfish, which was used to illustrate the sign of Cancer on medieval calendars.

– Choir stalls: eight of the ten misericords represent animals. Thus there is a lion devouring a lamb (medieval artisans often chose to illustrate fables and proverbs), a chained bear (a symbol of anger), a web-footed dragon, a cat lying in wait for a mouse, and a frog, among others.

PECULIAR MOTIFS UNDER THESE CANONS' SEATS!

Misericords are small sculptures beneath church stall folding seats that the monks can lean against, allowing them to appear to be standing when the seat is lifted. These objects, located as they are beneath the dignitaries' posteriors, could not represent sacred subjects or references. Medieval journeymen woodworkers thus jubilantly used this free space!

At both Saint Peter's Cathedral and Saint Gervais Temple – as well as in other churches of the Savoy dukedom – the misericords are a jumble of profane motifs that are often erotic or outright crude.

Thus there are devils, humans with animal ears, grimacing madmen and imaginary beasts. There are also lewd images, scenes of lust, and people contorting themselves in obscene positions.

Many of these misericords, probably the most outrageous ones, have disappeared or been damaged – the Reformation undoubtedly tried to tidy things up. It is also likely that the most provocative ones were simply taken by collectors.

Those remaining at Saint Peter's and Saint Gervais, many of which have been savagely attacked (masculine attributes were systematically targeted), allow visitors to imagine the profane creativity that slipped in beneath the canons' seats in 15th-century Geneva.

THE SIBYL OF SAINT PETER'S CATHEDRAL STALLS

Saint Peter's Cathedral
• Bus 36, Cathédrale stop

What is a woman, a pagan soothsayer, doing amongst the prophets and saints of the stalls of Saint Peter's? The sibyl of Eritrea is the last of a row of large figures carved in walnut and which dominate the seats once filled by the canons. The individuals venerated by Christianity are

> *A sibyl, or pagan soothsayer, honoured at Saint Peter's*

grouped according to the order established by the double Creed, or a prophet followed by a saint. Thus appear the prophet and King David, Saint Andrew, the prophet Isaiah, Saint James the Greater, the prophet Zachariah, Saint John the Evangelist, the prophet Hosea, Saint Thomas, the prophet Amos, and Saint James the Less. The sibyl is the eleventh figure. Originally, the prophet Jeremiah and Saint Peter were at the beginning of the row, but their stalls disappeared in the 17th century.

The sibyl of Eritrea was not the only one at Saint Peter's, however. Until the mid-18th century, there was a second row of stalls that also alternated prophets and saints. The sibyl of Tibur (now Tivoli, where her temple still stands; she supposedly slapped Christ during the Passion) stood at the end of the row.

This homage to sibyls, who preceded Christianity, intrigues visitors. They were, however, part of a long, post-Christian tradition and their *Sibylline Books* were adopted first by Judaism, then by Christianity, and used to facilitate the conversion of pagans to monotheism.

The sibyl of Saint Peter's Cathedral holds her book of oracles opened towards the viewer. Four nails are meant to hold the pages open. A text, undoubtedly acrostic verse, probably figured on these pages, but time has erased it. According to Eusebius, a Greek bishop, the Eritrean sibyl had foreseen the birth of Christ by placing the letters composing his name at the beginning of the lines of verse in which she gave her predictions: JESUS CHRISTUS SERVATOR CRUX.

The magnificent stalls of Saint Peter's have long intrigued art historians. At the end of the 20th century, there was still some debate as to whether they had been built for the cathedral or ordered for another Genevan church and transported to Saint Peter's after the Reformation. The hypothesis supported by Genevan Corinne Charles, published in 1999, seems to favour the first option.

SIBYLS: PROPHETS OF CHRIST?

Sibyls are the soothsayers of Antiquity, charged by Cybele, the mother goddess, to transmit their prophecies to the powerful, through the intermediary of *Oracles* and *Sibylline Books*, texts written in an enigmatic language allowing for numerous interpretations, which protected them from any subsequent disputes.

As they communicate with the divine, like prophets, sibyls are often considered to be a symbol of the Revelation.

Like the *Sibylline Books* sold to Romans (see below), twelve books, known as the *Sibylline Oracles*, began to circulate throughout the Mediterranean in the 3rd century BC. Some have survived to the present day, thanks to copies dating from the 15th and 16th centuries. According to the Roman Catholic Church, sibyls thus supposedly predicted the arrival of the Messiah and, in the 8th book, the Eritrean sibyl is also believed to have announced the second coming of Christ on Judgment Day.

In the 15th century, Dominican monk Filippo Barbieri helped to disseminate these books throughout Europe and, from then on, sibyls were abundantly represented in Western religious art. They were frequently shown facing the twelve prophets of the Old Testament, as in the Sistine Chapel in Rome, where the audacity of associating these ancient pagan divinities with the Revelation made to the prophets illustrates their adoption by the Catholic Church.

The adjective "sibylline", used to describe enigmatic (or ambiguous) writings and words, has its origin in the sibyls' oracles, which were open to numerous interpretations.

THE ROMANS, INTERPRETERS OF THE *SIBYLLINE BOOKS*

The Romans predicted the future in three ways: thanks to the omens, haruspices and the interpretation of the *Sibylline Books*. The six omens "took the auspices" (*aves spicere*: watch the birds) primarily by observing the flight of birds or the eating habits of sacred chickens.

The haruspices were priests of an inferior rank who studied the entrails (*hara* in Etruscan, according to some sources) of sacrifice victims in order to infer their omens.

Finally, Tarquinius Superbus (the 7th and last king of Rome, 535-509 BC), is believed to have bought three of the nine books by the Cumaean sibyl in order to find any indication of how to save Rome.

The word "sibyl" probably derives from Cybele, the mother goddess who charged the sibyls with transmitting prophecies, even if some scholars believe that the word is a corruption of the Sanskrit word *shramana*, or shaman, who also possessed the gift of predicting the future.

THE BOWED HEAD
OF THE PROPHET JEREMIAH

Saint Peter's Courtyard
• Bus 36, Cathédrale stop

> **Why isn't Jeremiah looking at the cathedral?**

L urking in a corner of Saint Peter's Courtyard is a statue of Jeremiah, the sorrowful prophet of the Book of Lamentations, placed here in 1938. Sculpted by Auguste de Niederhausen, this black, massive, and burdened Jeremiah seems to bear all the world's sorrows. He weeps over the taking of Jerusalem (607 BC).

Curiously, the statue is not looking at the cathedral, but faces the city instead, and thus looks at the faithful and not at the Temple. "Seeing it, you'd think it was Calvin fighting for the honour of God and the salvation of the Genevan people!" wrote one of the reformer's exegetes. Indeed, Calvin closely identified himself with the message transmitted by the prophet (*Sermons*, 1549; and *Lessons*, 1560-1563). This Jeremiah thus symbolizes a path to God, filled with humility and accessible to human beings, towards whom the statue faces.

AUGUSTE DE NIEDERHAUSEN, ONE OF RODIN'S STUDENTS

Born in 1863 at Vevey, Auguste de Niederhausen was a student of Rodin, which is the origin of his artistic name, "Rodo". His career was filled with heartbreak. Most of the art competitions in which he participated only disillusioned him. A friend of Verlaine, he completed several busts of the poet, one of which is in the Luxembourg Gardens in Paris. The artist was often misunderstood, and even mocked, as illustrated by this quatrain about the Saint Peter's statue:
"Do you know why Jeremiah
Was gloomy all his life?
Because the prophet predicted
That Rodo would do his portrait."
He has received due recognition since, however. His work is an important link between Rodin's lyrical work and modern sculpture. Auguste de Niederhausen sculpted "with his fists", as he used to say. He died poor in 1913. The Museum of Art and History owns seventy-three of his sculptures.

THE MYSTERIOUS HEADS OF THE TAVEL HOUSE

28

6, rue du Puits-Saint-Pierre
• Bus 36, Hôtel-de-Ville stop

*Attached
to a stunning
mauve façade*

Since the 14th century, ten heads have cheerfully and mischievously surveyed passers-by from the façade of the Tavel House.

What do they represent? Historians only have a few hypotheses: perhaps they are the portraits of the first owners, the heroes of some medieval novel, or perhaps simply an addition made by a talented stone carver?

Unfortunately, over six centuries, pollution slowly wore them away to the point that, today, only copies embellish the façade. The restored originals are on display inside.

There is another intriguing detail: what was the purpose of the iron supports holding heavy rings that are scattered along the façade? It is assumed that they must have held the poles from which canvases or canopies were hung in front of the windows.

The Tavel House, which probably dates from the 12th century, is the oldest preserved private residence in Geneva. In 1334, a major fire ravaged three-quarters of the upper city and reconstruction took several years. On this occasion, two corner turrets were added to the Tavel House, giving it its massive appearance. The rich and influential Tavel family played a large role in the city, but eventually died out in the 15th century. The house then had a number of rich owners, until it fell into the hands of the Calandrini family, who completely transformed it in the 17th century. One of the turrets was torn down, a monumental flight of steps was built, and, most importantly, the house acquired its characteristic mauve colour.

The residence was listed as a historic monument in 1923 and the city bought it in 1963, then restored it and converted it into a museum in 1986. The museum recreates the ambiance and living conditions of Genevans, from the Middle Ages to the beginning of the 1900s.

The showpiece of the Tavel House is a 30m^2 zinc and copper model of Geneva that shows the city as it was in the 1850s. The creation of architect Auguste Magnin, it is the result of over twenty years of hard work. This extraordinary record of the Geneva of yesteryear, sheltered behind its walls, will soon be digitized in 3-D.

THE LITTLE-KNOWN TRAVELS
OF FIVE ARSENAL CANNONS

Rue de l'Hôtel-de-Ville
• Bus 36, Hôtel-de-Ville stop

> *Taken by Napoleon, then the Austrians, a few pieces made it back to Geneva*

Although the site is an essential tourist stop, of the roughly 200 guns that once defended Geneva's walls, the cannons that have survived hold secrets that few locals know.

When the city was under the domination of Napoleon (1798-1813), the emperor requisitioned the majority of this artillery. The Austrians under general Bubna, having dislodged the French garrison, took the eighty-two remaining cannons with them when they left Geneva in early 1814.

Lieutenant Joseph Pinon then moved heaven and earth to retrieve the Genevan artillery. Throughout 1814, he travelled from city to city pleading his case to princes and allied generals, and, in the end, his efforts were rewarded. Forty-eight cannons were recovered and returned in three convoys. The first ones returned to Geneva in glory on 31 December 1814, and the others arrived on 23 February and 18 April 1815. Then, as years went by, they were dispersed and melted down, particularly in 1852.

Only one cannon had never left the city, as it was hidden by a handful of patriots. Built in 1721 by Daniel Wyss and bored by Leuw, the barrel is supported by two monkeys and the knob features a monkey's head in relief.

In 1923, the Military Museum of Vienna agreed to return the last four cannons in their possession. They are also decorated with animals engraved in the bronze: wolves, lions and mastiffs symbolizing power and vigilance. Three of the cannons are the work of a Dresden artist, Georg Münch (1725). The fourth, by master foundryman Martin Emery, was cast in Geneva in 1680 and is decorated with dolphins.

These are the five cannons that now occupy the cobblestone floor of the former Arsenal.

Under the vaults, against the back wall, three large mosaics by Genevan painter Alexandre Cingria gleam. They depict Caesar's arrival in 58 BC, the Count of Geneva and medieval fairs, and the welcoming of Protestant refugees after the Revocation of the Edict of Nantes.

In the beginning, and then under the Romans, this site was an open-air market that was covered in the early 15th century. In 1588, arcades were added to act as a foundation for a wheat loft. Not until 1720 did the site gain a new function – an armoury – which it lost in 1877 when the Arsenal was transferred to Plainpalais.

THE TOWN HALL'S BENCH OF JUSTICE

2, rue de l'Hôtel-de-Ville
• Bus 36, Hôtel-de-Ville stop

> *The site of death sentences*

A tired passer-by who decides to take a rest on this stone bench in front of the town hall has no idea of sitting where, until 1829, merciless judges pronounced death sentences. There used to be a platform across from them, where the other participants (witnesses and the accused) would stand.

Of the very long list of those condemned, three great figures whose fates were sealed before this white stone bench stand out. Jacques Gruet was beheaded in 1547 in Champel for atheism and blasphemy, after confessing under torture. In his writings, *Clarissime lector*, he had exposed his moral and political ideas: the clergy (Calvin was clearly the main target) should not be involved in politics, moral censorship, or in civil justice – standards that were incompatible with the period. Then it was the turn of the Spaniard Michel Servet, the "heretic" (also according to Calvin!), to be condemned to death in 1553 and burnt alive at Champel.

Jean-Jacques Rousseau was luckier. When he was put on trial in 1762 for his writings which "aim to destroy the Christian religion and all governments", he was far away from Geneva... So, they made do with a public burning of a counterfeit copy of *Emile* and an abridged version of *The Social Contract*. The sentence was annulled by decree on 3 January 1791, thirteen years after Rousseau's death.

In a drawing by Pierre Escuyer (1749-1834), you can see where the tribunal used to be, next to the town hall, with its guardrails and four stone steps. Next to it was the iron collar or yoke, which was moved just across the street below the wheat market (which later housed the old Arsenal and where the cannons are today) in 1562.

JACQUES GRUET: THE AUTHOR OF THE OLDEST GENEVAN DOCUMENT IN PATOIS

Jacques Gruet holds his place in Genevan history for a notice written in the local Genevan dialect and posted at night on Calvin's pulpit at Saint Peter's. Indeed, this document (the Cantonal Archives hold the original) is the oldest known text in patois. With a few strong words, Gruet denounces and accuses: *Quin dyablo! Et to sut que cetou fottu pretre renia not vegnon ice mettre en ruyna. Apret qu'on a prou endura, on se revenge.* Which means: "Damnation! There is no doubt that these bloody renegade priests have come to ruin us. When we have endured enough, we revolt."
The rest of the vengeful notice ran along the same lines.

THE HORSEMAN'S RAMP AT THE TOWN HALL ③①

2, rue de l'Hôtel-de-Ville
• Bus 36, Hôtel-de-Ville stop

> *On horseback all the way to the third floor!*

For the rich and powerful in the 16th century, getting to the upper floors of a residence on horseback was not an insignificant question. In Europe, however, only a few creations permitting this feat are known to exist: the ramps at the Château of Amboise and the Louvre in France, the ramp of Saint Mark's Campanile in Venice (generally unknown – see our guide *Secret Venice*), and, finally, that of Geneva's town hall.

Designed by Genevan resident Pernet De Fosses, the construction of this large ramp paved with small round stones began in 1555 and was finished in 1578 by the Bogueret brothers (one of whom, Nicolas Bogueret, was later

killed in the Escalade of 1602). At the top, engraved on the columns of the third and last floor, the date "1578" can indeed be seen along with the word *achevé* (completed) and the initials "NB" and "JB", those of Nicolas and Jean Bogueret.

A witness of the time observed: "*Two people who left their home on horseback can ascend side-by-side to the edifice's summit without touching the ground. It is quite convenient for those suffering from gout. Many times have I seen mayor Andrion ride from his home directly to the Council's door on the first floor...*"

A Genevan specificity, the town hall is not the seat of the municipal authorities, as its name might suggest, but in fact is the seat of the two Councils of the Republic and Canton of Geneva: the Grand Council (legislative), and the State Council (executive).

INSCRIPTION AT PROMENADE DE LA TREILLE ㉜

• Bus 36, 3, 5, Croix-Rouge stop

Baudet Tower's mysterious Roman inscription

At the foot of Baudet Tower, right next to the gate to the terrace facing the Treille, a Latin inscription intrigues passers-by. You have to look closely, as its letters in the stone are slowly fading. The following words can still be made out: RVFIAE AQVILINAE CF AT.

This funerary inscription probably comes from a Roman necropolis that used to be located near Place Neuve. Over time, all the good cut stones were habitually taken to be used in new constructions. Builders of all periods believed nothing should be wasted – everything could be transformed and re-used.

Set here during the tower's construction in 1455, this 4 metre engraved stone was dedicated to the Manes (the gods of the ancestors) and bears the name of Rufia Aquilina Clarissima Femina, a woman of senatorial rank, whose memory is thus discreetly perpetuated here.

SAINT GERMAIN: GENEVA'S OLDEST CHURCH PAID THE TAX FOR THE CRUSADES

Saint Germain is the oldest church in Geneva. The first documents to mention it date from 1218 and indicate that, on the order of Philip Augustus, the ecclesiastical authorities of the Dauphiné Viennois province, which included Geneva, taxed the parishes of the region at a sum equal to one-twentieth of their revenue in order to fund the Crusades. Yet, of Geneva s seven parishes, Saint Germain holds second place on this list.

The origins of Saint Germain date back much further, however, and undoubtedly precede the construction of the first basilica of Saint Peter's by several centuries. The 1334 fire in the upper city did not spare it, but it was rebuilt in just a few years. From that moment on, it had an eventful history. During the Reformation (according to Rome, the last Catholic ceremony was held on 15 August 1535), the church was neglected in favour of the nearby cathedral. It then served as a warehouse, arsenal, wheat loft, meeting room for the regional council and ... a butcher's shop. Reclaimed by churchgoers, Saint Germain became the refuge of the "old" Genevan Catholics at the time of the 1871 schism caused by Pius IX's dogma on pontifical infallibility. When the Roman Church officially regained possession of its property in 1907, these liberal Catholics could not reasonably be displaced.

THE STATUE OF PICTET DE ROCHEMONT

Promenade de la Treille
• Bus 36, 3, 5, Croix-Rouge stop

> *A sheep farmer who became a diplomat*

Geneva owes a lot to him. Thanks to his diplomatic talents, Pictet de Rochemont, in the 19th century, succeeded in convincing the Confederation to accept the canton in its organization and persuaded the allied sovereigns to agree to the enlargement of the territory, to satisfy the demands of the Swiss people. His success at the Congresses of Paris (1814), Vienna (1815) and Turin (1816) was decisive. Charles Pictet de Rochement had already retired from the political world, however, when they came looking for him at his farm in Lancy. His great passion was raising Merino sheep. It was mayor Ami Lullin who came to beg him: *"Charles, abandon your fields, your corn and your sheep. Geneva needs you to find its new destiny!"*

Rochemont donned his frock coat again and travelled from one capital to another, negotiating and convincing. If they had let him continue, he could have extended the canton of Geneva all the way to the foot of the Jura Mountains and even taken part of Savoy! But the Genevan Protestants were afraid to absorb populations that included so many Catholics, who could challenge their supremacy.

His mission accomplished, Pictet de Rochemont returned to his plough and discussed planting and stockraising with his farmers in the local dialect. His statue on the Treille (the work of Peter Hartmann) shows him holding a treaty. The artist could have shown him petting a Merino ewe with the other hand. The portrait of this exceptional man would thus have been complete.

THE TREILLE BENCH

• Bus 36, 3, 5, Croix-Rouge stop

The world's longest bench?

The bench that was installed along the Promenande de la Treille in 1767 was a veritable symbol of peace. Before, this mound served as a stronghold and observation post; cannons were placed here. From this dominant position, troops could watch the advancing enemy (the Savoyards, of course!) from the moment they crossed the Arve or Rhône rivers. In the 18th century, as the military threat faded and new neighbourhoods were built below, blocking the view, the hill became a meeting site for the entire city. People did not walk along the lakeside, as paths had not yet been installed, but instead they strolled along this sunny esplanade sheltered by the buildings of the Old City.

The crowd was so dense that a single wooden bench – 120 metres long – was installed along the path. This was surely a world record, at least at the time, and no one has contested it since (see box below).

This bench that is so dear to Genevan residents is sometimes the object of debate in the press or in the Grand Council. All it takes is a touch-up of the paint to spark heated discussions that go on for weeks about the shade of green that was chosen or the weather-resistance of the varnish... How happy a country it must be if the maintenance of a public bench makes the front page of the papers!

IS THE WORLD'S LONGEST BENCH IN MARSEILLE, FRANCE?

Marseille is the other city claiming to possess the world's longest bench (see our guide *Marseille insolite et secrete*, available in French). Although the Kennedy Coast Road's bench is 2 kilometres long, it is not made in one piece, and its longest uninterrupted section has never really been measured.

Treille (climbing vine) Promenade clearly owes its name to the vines that had been grown here since time immemorial. They were mainly "hutins", vine stocks climbing on arbours. In the 16th century, the Republic bought this piece of land, uprooted the vines, and built a strong retaining wall to defend the access to the Old City.

THE TREILLE'S "OFFICIAL" CHESTNUT TREE ㉟

• Bus 36, Croix-Rouge stop

> *An official tree that announces the coming of spring!*

Geneva has an "official" tree. Every year, the Promenade de la Treille chestnut tree is in charge of officially announcing the arrival of spring.

Well-protected at the end of the promenade, near Baudet Tower, the opening of its first bud used to be welcomed with much fanfare in a period when people had the time to celebrate the simple joys of life. Official speeches, children's dances and band music celebrated the appearance of the first leaf.

Although now this event is simply mentioned in the press, it remains an important moment of Genevan life. The ceremony is carried out in great pomp, with a bailiff wearing a red and yellow cape who follows the *Sautier* of the Republic at a respectable distance.

Rigorously noted in the registers since 1808, first by an amateur observer and with regard to a tree located further to the west, and then officially since

1818, the date of spring's arrival in Geneva every year feeds the statistics. We thus know that the first day of spring can vary considerably from one year to another.

Sometimes the first bud opened in January, and sometimes at the end of April. Having such a witness to observe such phenomena as the advancement of global warming is a source of pride for Geneva.

Since the first "administrative" observations, three trees have been used: the first from 1818 to 1905, the second until 1928, and the present one since 1929.

THE "CRAZY CHESTNUT"

The little chestnut tree planted in 1968 competes with the official patriarch. One year, it budded and announced the arrival of spring in December! Since then, it has been nicknamed the "crazy chestnut".

THE *SAUTIER* OF THE REPUBLIC

The rue du Sautier (between Grand-Rue and Saint Germain Church) is a narrow alley that bears the name of a typically Genevan official. From the 6th century, the *sautier* was the head of the watchmen and the guardian of the town hall. The first person appointed to this position was Jean de Passy (1483-1496), and, of the seventy *sautiers* who followed him, the current one, Maria Anna Hutter, is only the second woman to hold this office. Today, as there are no more enemies to watch out for, she is the general secretary and director of the services of the Grand Council.

One of the most famous *sautiers* was Pierre Canal (1608-1610). His father, Jean, had been one of the heroes of the Escalade. Alas, the son was accused of being a spy for the court of Savoy. Arrested, then tortured, he confessed what they wanted him to confess and was condemned to be burned alive "slowly but surely" after first being hung from the gallows at Molard. With his last breath, he retracted his confessions, but that failed to shake the judges' convictions. His ashes were thrown into the Arve river.

Today, in addition to her other more serious responsibilities, the *sautier* must "watch out" for the apparition of the first leaf on the Treille's "official" chestnut tree. Beware the consequences to her reputation if she misses it!

WHERE DOES THE WORD *SAUTIER* COME FROM?

Etymologically, *sautier* comes from low Latin and means "he who guards the harvests" (from *saltus*, forest or lands). It is thus this meaning of "guardian" that first prevailed. Over time, this admittedly anachronistic, yet picturesque, term was kept.

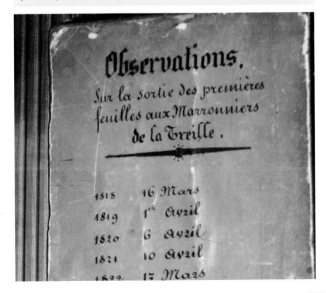

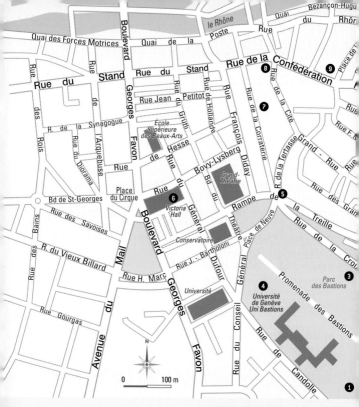

LOWER CITY

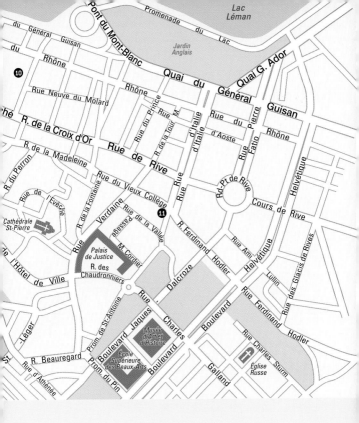

THE ANGEL OF THE MONUMENT TO THE RED CROSS CENTENARY

1

Parc des Bastions
• Bus and trams: stops in front of the Grand Théâtre

> *An unloved statue...*

Away from the main paths of Bastions park, strollers may stumble across a group of sculptures. An angel, as hefty as a rugby player with one arm bent and raised in a strange movement (a gesture often misinterpreted by jocular visitors...), is meant to protect the frightened figures behind. He has his back turned to a dying soldier and refugees looking for shelter. The jury undoubtedly misunderstood this ambiguous attitude. In reality, the sculptor wanted to show the angel addressing the Creator and interceding on behalf of war victims.

This work by Jacques Probst was first intended to stand along the Promenade de la Treille, a well-exposed and popular site. Disappointed by the result, the committee and the city probably judged this massive composition to be too "modern" and the sculpture was ultimately relegated to this corner of Bastions park, which is more popular with pigeons than with visitors.

The monument was commissioned for the centennial of the International Committee of the Red Cross (ICRC), and was erected in 1963 thanks to fundraising that resulted in the collection of 200,000 Swiss francs.

HENRY DUNANT: "INITIATOR", "PROMOTER", OR "FOUNDER" OF THE RED CROSS?

An inscription on the base of the sculpture describes Henry Dunant as the "initiator" of the work of the ICRC. Curiously, on the plaque his family paid to have placed at number 12, rue Verdaine in 1919 (where he was born in 1828), he is called the "promoter" of the Red Cross. Finally, on the monument stele beneath his bust on Place Neuve, inaugurated in 1980 (see page 103), he is attributed the role of "founder"...

The evolution of these appellations illustrates how the perception of his role evolved over time, and how grudges that hindered his being officially recognized by Genevans – his debts, bankruptcy, and forced exile – slowly dissipated.

Railings have surrounded the Bastions park since 1864. From time to time there is a public outcry to remove them, as the regular maintenance of this wrought iron artwork runs into millions and most of the railings around other Genevan parks (notably the Jardin Anglais, Perle du Lac and Parc Bertrand) were removed some seventy years ago.

OLD GENEVA'S UNDERGROUND TUNNELS

Built along the periphery of the Old City beneath the former fortifications, the network of underground tunnels is one of Geneva's great "secrets". Few residents would ever suspect the existence of these tunnels running beneath their streets.

The tunnels served two purposes. On the one hand, they were used to transport explosives discreetly beneath the exterior structures, explosives that could be ignited if ever the enemy took control. On the other hand, they allowed soldiers to move quietly between the various defensive bastions.

Drawn up in 1720, the map of this network was transmitted to the military headquarters of Grenoble when Geneva was annexed to France in 1798. Unfortunately, the map was misplaced, even if, at the time of the Restoration in 1814, a copy was given to the Genevan authorities. But this copy was lost yet again in 1857!

Genevan historian Louis Blondel became fascinated by the subject. Thanks to him, most of this network of tunnels was redrawn. Without going into the ramifications of this rather complex map, we can say that there is a deep "main tunnel" starting at rue Pierre-Fation, going up towards rue Sturm, Tœpffer square, and Terrasse Saint-Victor, and then descending beneath Charles-Bonnet square, cours des Bastions, boulevard Helvétique, rue de Candolle, rue Saint-Léger, boulevard des Philosophes and regaining rue de Candolle, opposite the east wing of the university. The largest branch of this main tunnel measured 138 metres and ended at the top of route de Florissant.

These tunnels were solid and rather wide, with brick vaults resting on a foundation of rolled hardcore. Most of them have been filled in or their entries blocked and forgotten. However, it is possible to advance several hundred metres along the "listening gallery" (which connected the Saint-Léger entrance to the one on rue du Vieux-Collège), by entering via the basement of the Museum of Art and History (see photo below).

The underground network was about 5 kilometres long, without counting the twenty-seven blockhouses built along boulevard des Casemates and boulevard Helvétique, which were linked to the parallel explosives tunnel by two sets of eleven steps.

Below rue de la Croix-Rouge, which used to be part of a defensive wall between the Oie and Saint-Léger bastions, there is a vaulted gallery whose entrance was in the garden of Eynard Palace, next to the Mirond bastion (see photo opposite).

JULIETTE DROUET NAKED

Pedestal of the bust of Augustin-Pyrame de Candolle
Parc des Bastions
• Bus 36, Croix-Rouge stop

> *Victor Hugo's lover dances at Parc des Bastions*

A distracted visitor would not linger around the bust of Augustin-Pyrame de Candolle in the Bastions park. Of course, this august personage is the founder of the Botanical Gardens. In 1818, he planted a wide range of rare plants in this formerly marshy area. The arboretum was transferred in 1904 to a larger terrain, on route de Lausanne, at the edge of the city.

The décor engraved on the pedestal is interesting, however. There are four scantily or unclad female dancers, surrounded by chubby-cheeked cherubs, who merrily dance around the rather severe bust.

A literature buff curiously enough might recognize Juliette Drouet, the celebrated lover of Victor Hugo.

At the time, she was the mistress of sculptor James Pradier. She even had a daughter by him, Claire, in 1828. Pradier, who perhaps had doubts about the baby's paternity, turned out mother and daughter in an act that infuriated his friend Victor Hugo, who forced Pradier to legally recognize little Claire two years later. Hugo, who had become Juliette's new lover in the meantime, became Claire's godfather.

Juliette Drouet was also depicted by James Pradier on the statue symbolizing Strasbourg on Place de la Concorde in Paris.

WHAT BECAME OF JAMES PRADIER?

Attracted by young girls throughout his life, James Pradier died of a heart attack at the age of 62, in 1852, while picnicking in the company of Adeline, a 16-year-old adolescent.

THE LITTLE SECRETS
OF THE REFORMATION WALL

3

Parc des Bastions
• Tram 17, Bus 1, Place Neuve stop

*It was
never
finished...*

Against the Treille's old walls in the Bastions park, the immense sculpted fresco of the Reformation Wall is, of course, well-known by Geneva's inhabitants, even if many of them have a little trouble naming, in order, the four large stone figures that stand in the centre of the composition: Farel, Calvin, Bèze and Knox.

The reason for its location, on the other hand, is much less well-known. In 1908, the buttresses of the old fortifications urgently needed to be consolidated, so a competition was launched and seventy-one propositions were submitted. The Lausanne architects who presented this project of a roughly 100 metre wall carried off the prize by cleverly combining utility with a homage to the most glorious reformers.

In fact the Reformation Wall was never really finished. According to the original plans, the figures of Pierre Olivétan, a cousin of Calvin who evangelized the canton of Vaud, and Thomas Cranmer, the first reformed archbishop of England, were supposed to be included in the lateral bas-reliefs. Two other glorious Protestants, John Wycliffe and Jan Hus, were entitled to just two modest inscriptions, although initially they were to receive much greater honours.

The rapid finishing of the construction, after eight years of work, was undoubtedly linked to the uncertainty of the period. In August 1917, the date of the inauguration, the First World War had mobilized many workers.

LANDOWSKI: THE SCULPTOR OF THE REFORMATION WALL...
AND THE CHRIST OF RIO DE JANEIRO!

The "Christ the Redeemer" that has dominated Rio's bay from its 30 metre height since 1931 has a familial link to the stone reformers of the Bastions park. Indeed, it is the work of sculptor Paul Landowski and his collaborator, Henri Bouchard, who also created the statues of Geneva's wall.

DAVID, VAINQUEUR DE GOLIATH STATUE ❹

Parc des Bastions
• Tram 17, Bus 1, Place Neuve stop

> *An offended sculptor...*

Often intriguing to visitors because there is no sign to identify it, the sculpture of *David, Conqueror of Goliath*, which sits imposingly in the Bastions park, is the last work by Jean-Étienne Chaponnière. It was awarded the gold medal at the Paris Art Salon of 1835, shortly before the artist's death from tuberculosis at the age of 34.

The young sculptor was already known to the public and his career was very promising. In 1833, most notably, Auguste Thiers had commissioned him to complete one of the four bas-reliefs of the Triumphal Arch in Paris – *The Fall of Alexandria by General Kleber*. It stands near the more famous bas-reliefs by Rude, Cortot and Etex.

The Bastions park statue – not far from the Place Neuve entrance – apparently caused some controversy at the time of its installation. Indeed, his

first version showed David wearing a bearskin. A jealous colleague mocked this attire, claiming that Chaponnière was using it to hide his inability to sculpt the human body. Cut to the quick, the artist thus created a second version, the one that visitors can now admire in the Bastions park.

Cast in bronze for Geneva, the statue was placed here in 1854. His foot placed victoriously on the giant's head, David leans against a heavy sword that he would likely have trouble brandishing... But there will be no third version.

SCULPTORS WHO CHANGE THEIR FIRST NAME...

Jean-Étienne Chaponnière chose the name John when he turned 21. He thus followed the fashion of the period and imitated his master, Pradier, who changed his name from Jean-Jacques to James.

THE CURIOUS LOCATION
OF THE BUST OF HENRY DUNANT

⑤

Place Neuve
• Bus 3, 5, 9, tram 12, Place Neuve stop

> *The founder of the Red Cross waited 70 years before being honoured by his home town!*

Henry Dunant had a lot of trouble obtaining homage from the Genevans. Many of them, it is true, had been ruined in the bankruptcy of the Crédit Genevois bank, of which he was one of the administrators.

Dishonoured and condemned, Dunant was able to flee to France thanks to his double nationality. He was 39 years old and he would never again set foot in his home town.

The founder of the Red Cross, who died in 1910, still had no statue in 1980, when a group of citizens collected 14,000 francs to erect a bust in this corner of Place Neuve. In 1919, however, Henry Dunant's nephew had already attempted to erect a commemorative monument and had asked the Genevan government for aid. The Grand Council's refusal was bitter.

The site where the bust was placed is also where executions used to be carried out. It was chosen as a reminder that Henry Dunant had also vehemently fought against the death penalty. Dunant, a man who followed his convictions, had been traumatized on witnessing a failed hanging in 1862.

The bust on Place Neuve shows Henry Dunant wearing a moustache, sideburns, and a bow tie. This sober image is meant to honour the Nobel Peace Prize recipient (1901), and not the young colonist who pursued perilous business dealings in Algeria and got up to his eyes in debt (the concession he had obtained, including a farm and windmills, collapsed, leading to his ruin... and some embezzlement).

THE GUILLOTINE IN GENEVA

On 31 March 1800, the date of the second execution by guillotine in Geneva, this sinister device was installed at the site where Dunant's bust now stands. The blade and lunette are kept in Tavel House museum. The last execution took place in 1862.

THE NAKED STATUE OF "HARMONY" AT VICTORIA HALL

❻

Victoria Hall
14, rue du Général-Dufour
• Tram 14, Cirque stop
• Bus 5, Place Neuve stop

> *Immodesty that caused a scandal*

Although nowadays Genevan residents walk past Victoria Hall without raising their heads, this was not always the case.

When the auditorium was inaugurated on 28 November 1894, the allegorical statue of "Harmony", shown life-size and entirely naked, attracted quite a few ribald looks. Before then, statues of unclothed women generally hid the "strategic" spot through the positioning of the knee, a modest hand, or even a providential branch. This time, the woman brazenly exposed her anatomy. Sculptor Joseph Massaerotti, who had worked according to a model by Parisian artist Jean Coulon, thus had his hour of glory. A different time, a different turmoil! Nevertheless, the public became so accustomed to this provocative nudity that, in 1896, Pastor Frank Thomas organized a series of sermons at Victoria Hall. His sermons drove away licentious ideas...

Thanks to an Englishman's passion for the concerts given on boats sailing on Lake Geneva, Victoria Hall was built here between 1891 and 1894. Daniel Barton had come to Geneva to learn to manage his immense fortune and had set up the Nautical Band in 1883. This orchestra was meant to enliven the regattas of which Barton was so fond, as well as the other events of the Nautical Society.

The orchestra needed an auditorium, however, as the boat decks could only be used in the summer. In honour of his wife, Victoria-Alexandra, and of Queen Victoria (a strong diplomatic double whammy – Barton was vice-consul of Great Britain), he thus had Victoria Hall built. The building, which possesses exceptional acoustics, could hold 1,800 music lovers, a record for Geneva at the time.

In 1905 (Barton died in 1907), Victoria Hall was bequeathed to the City of Geneva.

In 1915, the Nautical Band received the title of Municipal Orchestra. Today, it is called the City of Geneva Wind Ensemble.

On 16 September 1984, a fire ravaged the auditorium, partly destroying the interior décor. After restoration, Victoria Hall was added to the cantonal list of protected monuments in 1986.

The auditorium Visitors' Book contains many famous signatures, including those of Saint-Saëns, Vincent d'Indy, Grieg, Rubinstein, Reineke and Massenet.

THE GROTESQUE FIGURE OF RUE DE LA CORRATERIE

7, rue de la Corraterie
• Trams 12, 17, Bel-Air stop

At number 7, rue de la Corraterie, a grotesque figure placed as the keystone above the door intrigues passers-by. Who is this woman wearing a cap and a collar? Is it Lady Piaget, who threw the key to her alley to the defenders of Geneva during the Escalade of 1602 before barricading herself in her room, finding the strength to push a vast wardrobe in front of the door?

Mère Royaume: Geneva's most famous heroine was from Lyon, France

Or is it Mère (Mother) Royaume, a 60-year-old woman from Lyon, mother of sixteen, who entered Geneva's history books when she stunned a Savoyard soldier by throwing a heavy pewter cauldron at him? Tradition has preferred the latter interpretation. It is true that Mother Royaume assures the income of Geneva's confectioners, who make thousands of chocolate cauldrons filled with marzipan vegetables in her memory.

The Corraterie – where the horse dealers let the horses "run" – runs alongside the vestiges of the old walls of the upper city. A plaque reminds visitors that this is where the Genevans pushed back the Savoyards during the memorable Escalade, forcing them into a mad rush back down their ladders.

The Corraterie was drastically changed and realigned countless times. The buildings that were destroyed over time (notably Thellusson Tower) gave way to buildings whose pediments were designed by Dufour, an engineer and general, in 1825. A few prestigious shops are located here.

THÉODORE DE BÈZE ON THE ESCALADE FOUNTAIN

8

Corner of rue de la Cité and rue de la Confédération
• Trams 12, 16, 17, Bel-Air stop

> *In fact, de Bèze didn't even wake up for the attack...*

One of the two bronze bas-reliefs of the Escalade fountain at the lower end of rue de la Cité shows Théodore de Bèze celebrating the victory at Saint Peter's Cathedral. However, legend says the old reformer was a little hard-of-hearing – he was 83 years old – and, in fact, didn't even wake up for the attack. What is certain is that it was not him, but Pastor Antoine de la Faye, who briefly interpreted Psalm 214 at 8am on Sunday in the cathedral, and that the morning services could not be held.

When he made this monument in 1857, sculptor Johan Leeb of Munich disregarded historical truth and followed tradition, sculpting Théodore de Bèze thanking God surrounded by a crowd of believers.

The basin of the fountain is sculpted in granite taken from an erratic boulder found nearby in Esery, France. The Savoyard workers, who learned a little too late what it was to be used for, shouted that if the stone wasn't so heavy they would take it back immediately!

The other bas-relief depicts a combat scene, with the heroines Lady Piaget and Mother Royaume appearing in the background.

WHY WAS THE ESCALADE FOUNTAIN PLACED SO FAR FROM THE SITE OF THE SAVOYARD ATTACK THAT WAS MIRACULOUSLY REPELLED IN 1602?

The Escalade fountain owes its location at the lower end of rue de la Cité to the fact that this is where one of the noble Savoyards, François de Sonnaz, after having cleared the wall near the Corraterie with seven scouts, turned back to announce to the attackers that "Geneva is sleeping and doesn't suspect a thing!". Unfortunate Sonnaz – he had only a few more hours to live before being hung, despite the large ransom (his weight in silver) that he offered to save his skin.

THE FORGOTTEN ORIGIN
OF THE RUES-BASSES LIONS

❾

5, rue de la Confédération
• Trams 12, 16, 17, Bel-Air stop

The enormous lions supporting the balcony at the entrance of number 5, rue de la Confédération – in Rues-Basses – were placed here at the beginning of the 20th century by the sculptor Jacques during

> *Symbol*
> *of a distant family*
> *of ambassadors*

construction work on the shopping arcade that was cut through this then rundown block by architect Adrien Peyrot. They perpetuate the memory of the lions which, in the 16th century, adorned the Chapeaurouge residence, a family of ambassadors of which the king of animals was the symbol.

On photographs predating 1906, thus taken before the demolitions that transformed the entire sector, a small lion can be seen lying on the façade of the old Bautte house, in an interior courtyard.

The *Lion d'Or* (Golden Lion) hotel, which later occupied this site,

also undoubtedly inherited the symbol of the Chapeaurouge family and gave its name to the covered passage connecting Rues-Basses to number 4, rue du Rhône.

The *Tour Perse* (Persian Tower), a famous inn where people of quality stayed (reformer Farel was in residence here in 1532), was also located at this address.

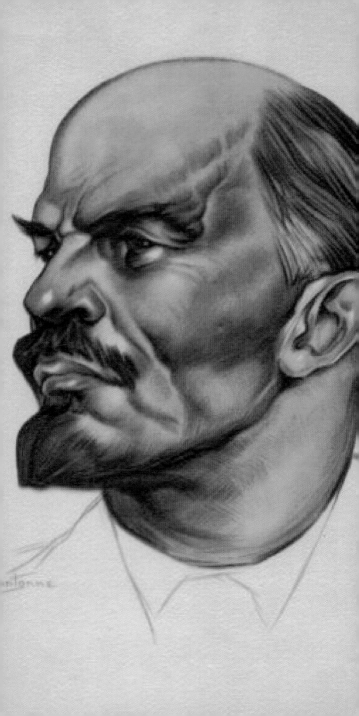

A CONTROVERSIAL BAS-RELIEF AT MOLARD 🔟

Molard Tower
• Trams 12, 16, 17, Place du Molard stop

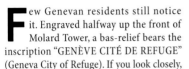

*Lenin,
a symbol
for refugees?*

Few Genevan residents still notice it. Engraved halfway up the front of Molard Tower, a bas-relief bears the inscription "GENÈVE CITÉ DE REFUGE" (Geneva City of Refuge). If you look closely, you can see that it depicts the Republic welcoming into its protective arms a person who is no other than... Lenin.

Built in 1591, Molard Tower has been restored several times. The last renovation dates back to 1906-1907, a period during which the Russian revolutionary paraded his incipient baldness and his goatee through Geneva's influential circles. Lenin, a political exile, spent long periods in Geneva, particularly in 1903-1905 and 1907-1908. This bas-relief was added in 1920.

As no inscription indicates that the model for the individual was indeed Lenin, one wonders why this information isn't provided. Is this discretion due to the controversial decision to make Lenin the symbol of the thousands of refugees Geneva has welcomed over the centuries? Some Genevans, who would have preferred that another illustrious refugee be chosen for this homage – and there are many! – have sometimes taken the choice to be a provocation...

Lenin arrived in Switzerland after having spent three years imprisoned in Siberia, and it was there that his conception of the revolutionary party matured. A commemorative plaque has been placed on the residence where he stayed at the time, at number 5, rue Plantaporrêts.

WHERE DOES THE WORD "MOLARD" COME FROM?
The lake used to come up to this point and, until the beginning of the 19th century, there was a merchant port here. "Molard" comes from the French word *mole* (pier), referring to the jetty that protected the entrance to the port.

EN TIU DOMO LOĜIS EN 1905
L. L. ZAMENHOF, INICIATORO
DE LA LINGVO ESPERANTO

THE PLAQUE TO THE CREATOR OF ESPERANTO

⓫

12, rue du Vieux-Collège
• Bus 8, tram 16, Rive stop

> *"... not because it brought the minds of men closer, but because it brought their hearts closer"*

In the very busy rue du Vieux-Collège, a discreet marble plaque has been erected on a section of wall at the entrance to an ivy-covered staircase leading to rusted and locked iron gates.

The inscription, in a bizarre language that is half-familiar and half-strange, indicates that this is where Ludovic Lazarus Zamenhof, the "initiator of the Esperanto language", once lived.

Born in 1859 in a small town in Russian Poland that was home to Germans, Poles, Russians and Jews, Zamenhof was faced with the puzzle of languages at an early age, hence his burning desire to dedicate his life to inventing a common language for all humanity.

A fact that is often ignored, it was as a pioneer of Progressive Education (a movement that is still strongly active and one of the goals of which is to promote world peace) that Zamenhof conceived Esperanto.

In 1887, he finally succeeded in publishing a brochure providing the bases of a universal language. He signed it as "Doctor Esperanto" (he who hopes). As years went by, Zamenhof gathered more and more followers across Europe and America, and his conferences reunited thousands of enthusiasts.

After Boulogne-sur-Mer (1905), he arrived in Geneva the following year. At Victoria Hall, he declared: "The first Esperantists loved Esperanto, not because it brought the minds of men closer, but because it brought their hearts closer." This key statement brought a standing ovation!

In 1914, the conference was supposed to be held in Paris in the month of August. On his way to France, Zamenhof was blocked in Cologne, Germany. For days, he watched columns of soldiers crossing the Rhine. "The vision of combat rose in front of his eyes. He had arrived too late with his dream of peace and universal brotherhood. Something in him shattered."

Zamenhof died in 1917 without having seen the end of the war.

In the first half of the 19th century, an Englishman, Peter Mark Roget, the son of Pastor John Roget of Geneva, had also launched a project for an artificial language meant to serve as a common language for all the peoples on Earth. Having become a reputable doctor and lexicographer, the author of the illustrious *Roget's Thesaurus of English Words and Phrases* (1852) quickly abandoned what was then considered to be a utopia.

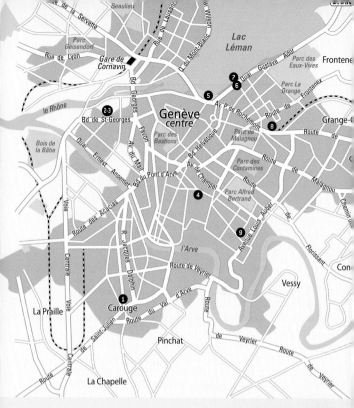

LEFT BANK

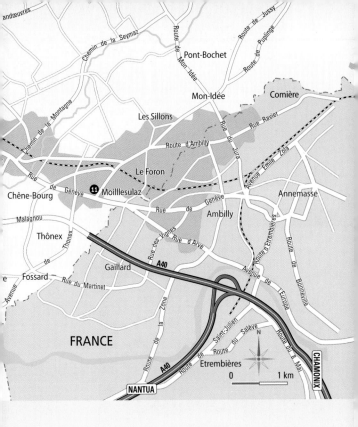

SECRET GARDENS OF CAROUGE

- Guided tours from June to October
- Contact Loredan Gianna: gianna@illico-travel.ch
- Tours: start at 11am. Duration: 75 minutes
- Fee: CHF 10 adults; CHF 5 children, students, teachers, unemployed
- Tel. 022 300 59 60
- Trams 13, 14, Place du Marché stop

> *Little gems you can visit*

Carouge possesses dozens of gardens hidden behind high walls or concealed in inner courtyards. Mainly private and jealously guarded, they are nevertheless accessible through organized tours that allow enthusiasts to discover these little gems. This profusion of gardens stems from the design of the area, which was built in the second half of the 18th century by the architects in the service of the kingdom of Sardinia. The idea was to build a city (Carouge had only seventeen houses) to compete with Geneva, on the other bank of the Arve River. Five blueprints were drawn up between 1772 and 1783, with the grid pattern of one- and two-storey buildings emerging as the favourite. Most of them kept green areas behind the façades facing the street. These secret gardens are all different. Some are rather large, others minuscule; some are well-kept, while others are left in poetic abandon... Whether they are perfectly maintained or have become islands in the urban jungle, they all charm visitors with their spontaneity and serve as a buffer from the noise of the city.

Some of the gardens have even been made "official", like that of the town hall. It nevertheless has kept its confidentiality – you can only reach it by going through the back garden of the administrative offices.

HOLY CROSS CHURCH DID A U-TURN

There is still a rivalry between Catholic Carouge and Protestant Geneva! In 1777, architect Giuseppe-Battista Piacenza was commissioned to build Holy Cross Church. The kingdom of Sardinia's objective was to construct a sort of Counter-Reformation cathedral. The plans included a choir turned away from place du Marché, with the nave extending onto place de Sardaigne. A first section was blessed in 1780 (religious constructions took time...). In 1824, after Carouge had been joined with Geneva – the Treaty of Turin had been signed eight years earlier – the construction had progressed so little that everything could still be changed. Architect Louis Bugatti took over the project and reversed the initial plan! The church, which is the canton's only example of Baroque religious architecture, thus had its entrance towards place du Marché. Today, who would suspect this long-ago U-turn?

AN EMBLEMATIC CINEMA SAVED BY LOCAL WILLPOWER

The Bio cinema is so strongly connected to the heritage of Carouge's inhabitants that they fought like lions when they feared it would disappear. In 2004, the town was thus able to buy it and a foundation then came up with novel solutions to renovate it entirely and make it financially viable. The most spectacular idea was to let sympathizers sponsor one of the new seats, each of which would bear the name of an international film celebrity. Thus, for a thousand franc donation, you could have your name – or that of your business – placed next to that of Alain Delon, Marilyn Monroe or Marlon Brando… Another idea to bring in money: the old seats were sold to film buffs, and today these chairs redolent with history can be found in local businesses or sitting imposingly in the living rooms of local residents.

But why is it called the "Bio"? It has nothing to do with biology or the biography of Carougian cinema, even if you have to look into that to find the explanation. The cinema had many names: the Ideal-Cinéma in 1912, Chanteclair-Cinéma in 1913-1915, Cinéma-Carouge in 1920, Carouge-Cinéma in 1928-1951, and then the Vox from 1952 to 1971. However, this last name had one major fault in the eyes of the owners: as the cinema listings were given in alphabetical order in the newspaper programme, the Vox was always at the very bottom…

In 1972, they thus had the idea of naming the cinema after the first cinematographic device perfected by Georges Demény and used by the Lumière brothers – the Biographe, which was shortened to "Bio" by the Carougians.

47, rue Saint-Joseph. Trams 13, 14, Marché stop

BIO FOR BIOGRAPHE, GEORGES DEMÉNY'S INVENTION

Georges Demény needs us to remember his contribution to the seventh art, because he is a forgotten figure in the history of cinema. Of Hungarian origin but born in Douai, France, he developed the Phonoscope (1891), then the Chronophotographe with an eccentric cam (1894) that allowed

movement to be broken down and analysed thanks to a successive series of photographs.

Sent to Sweden on a mission, his Chronophotographe – which had become the Biographe – had great success, which explains why Swedes still say "I'm going to the Bio".

CEMETERY OF THE KINGS, PLAINPALAIS   ❷

• Bus 32, Savoises stop

J ohn Calvin died on the evening of Saturday, 27 May 1564. He was only 55 years old, but he was already an old man suffering from ulcers, gout, rheumatism and kidney stones...

Calvin's fake grave

Scorning earthly honours, he had requested to be buried in a virtually anonymous way, without speeches or hymns, and, most importantly, he did not want the location of his grave to be marked.

Enveloped in coarse fabric, his body was buried at Plainpalais Cemetery. Where? No one knows.

Not until 1840, 276 years after his death, was a stone the size of a shoebox and bearing the initials J.C. placed at the presumed site of his grave, beneath one of the four willow trees which, according to tradition, were planted on his grave.

In truth, Calvin must have been buried in the area which, at the time, was reserved for religious ministers and professors, at the foot of the wall against which ancient tombstones lean (at right angles to this tomb).

In 1999, flouting the wishes of the great Reformer, which had been respected for more than four centuries, an elected official who wanted to attract tourists, and despite fierce protestations from hard-line Genevan residents, had wrought-iron railings placed around the supposed grave. The J.C. stone was moved and centred on the grave, low bushes were planted, and flagstones were installed so curious visitors wouldn't have to walk in the mud. A plaque bearing a detailed inscription was added – everything Calvin had dreaded...

SIGHTS NEARBY   ❸

THE GRAVE OF GRISÉLIDIS RÉAL, GENEVA S MOST FAMOUS PROSTITUTE

About 30 metres from Calvin's grave is that of Grisélidis Réal, the most famous Genevan prostitute and author of *La Passe imaginaire* (a collection of letters she wrote to a friend – *la passe* is French slang for the short time spent with a prostitute). In 2009, the transfer of her remains to Plainpalais Cemetery, the Genevan Pantheon, caused quite a stir.

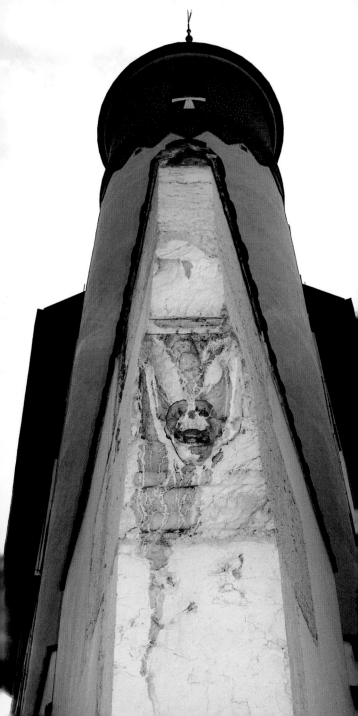

THE MASONIC BLAVIGNAC TOWER

1, rue de la Tour
• Bus 1, Lombard stop

"The strongest tower is the name of God"

Blavignac Tower was nearly demolished in 1965 when the City of Geneva acquired it with plans to redevelop the neighbourhood. A surge of historic preservation finally led to its complete restoration in 1995-1997.

Blavignac Tower was an architectural wager. Building such a structure on so narrow a plot – a polygonal plan in a corner shape – was risky. Jean-Daniel Blavignac, the famous architect who notably participated in the restoration of Saint Peter's cathedral, ruined himself building it, in fact, from 1859 to 1862.

Blavignac was a tormented soul. A Protestant, he turned to Roman Catholicism, which he renounced before dying in 1876. He became a Freemason, enrolling at the Prudence and Fidelity lodge. His tower is thus riddled with Masonic symbols. Under the windows, elaborate eaves and keystones can be found the set square and five-pointed star.

The pediment of a door is also engraved with a phrase framed by two small Templar crosses pattée: *Turris Fortissima Nomen Domini* ("The strongest tower is the name of God"). This man fascinated by heraldry searched for God all his life, turning from men, an attitude that ultimately brought him the

most extreme solitude before his death at 59.

Originally, the tower was more than just a Masonic meeting site. It also held housing and businesses. Fragments of an inscription above a door facing the street indicate that a Boulangerie de la Tour (Tower Bakery) was located here in 1867.

Today, a *Maison de quartier* (local social centre) occupies part of Blavignac Tower.

THE SAVOYARD WOMEN OF THE NATIONAL MONUMENT ❺

Quai du Général-Guisan
• Bus 8, 9, 27, Jardin Anglais stop

Sculptor Robert Dorier should have been more careful. By choosing buxom Savoyard women as the models symbolizing the union of Geneva and Switzerland, he should have known that the secret would leak out sooner or later and they would be laughed to scorn. Taking the representatives of the secular enemy to erect this national monument was ill-advised indeed.

Savoyard women represent Geneva and Switzerland!

Robert Dorier was born in 1830 in Baden, in the canton of Aargau. As his career partly developed in France (in Père-Lachaise Cemetery, Paris, the tomb of national guard Constant Séraphin Demion is thus decorated with a medallion signed by Robert Dorier), it seems he Frenchified his original name, changing it from "Dorer" to "Dorier". It is also probable that Dorier had simply kept his habitual Savoyard models when he was commissioned to do the Genevan statues, hoping that this "detail" wouldn't be discovered...

The sculpture was inaugurated at the Jardin Anglais, behind the Flower Clock, on 20 September 1869, five years after the original inauguration date. The delay was caused by grave disturbances that broke out the day before the first official ceremony as a result of a fixed election.

PRIVATE BOAT TRIP ON THE "NEPTUNE" ❻

Quai marchand des Eaux-Vives (left bank)
Fondation Neptune
Department of Territory, Nature and Environment, 7 rue des Battoirs,
1205 Geneva
• Tel. +41 022 388 55 44
• For hire from CHF 1,000 for 3 hours

Sail on Lake Geneva as in days gone by

Every time the "Neptune" sails away from Geneva's piers and unfurls its white sails, it is a celebration. This majestic boat (27.3m long and 8.5m wide), built in 1904 in Locum, near Meillerie in the Haut-Lac region, was used to transport stones and construction materials. It was saved in 1971 and bought by the Genevan government.

In 1972, while discussions regarding its fate were still ongoing, the Neptune sank due to water that had seeped into its rotting hull. Its most recent renovation (2.4 million francs) dates back to 2004-2005.

Since 2006, this superb boat has been available for hire for private events. The only stipulation is that, to sail, the capacity is limited to thirty-five people (ninety if the motor is used). Each year, the "Neptune" completes about a hundred paid excursions that can last from an hour to an entire day, which covers its operating and maintenance costs.

THE PIERRE DU NITON LANDMARK ❼

Quai Gustave-Ador
• Bus 9, 27, Pierre-Fatio stop. Bus 8, Place-du-Port stop

> *The official landmark of Swiss cartography*

Although the Pierres du Niton (Neptune's Stones) are well-known by Genevan residents, it is sometimes forgotten that the farthest away of the two erratic blocks jutting up about 2 metres in Geneva's harbour is the landmark used for all altimetric measurements in Switzerland. A bronze peg embedded in the flattest stone marks its altitude at 373.6m above sea-level (based on the average level of the Mediterranean). This Pierre du Niton owes the honour to Genevan engineer Guillaume-Henri Dufour (portrait below), who first used this geodesic mark to align and construct the Gustave-Ador pier along the lake. A few years later

(1820), having become a colonel in the Swiss army, Dufour again used the landmark to draw up a series of maps of Switzerland. At the time, the Pierre du Niton's altitude of reference was 376.86m. The measurement was corrected in 1902 when it was recalculated by J. Hifiker. In fact, the altitude of this landmark was measured several times in the 19th century on the basis of surveying work carried out by France from the Marseille tide gauge, the point of reference for French altimetry. Geneva thus had to be lowered by 3.26m!

WHEN GARGANTUA SKIPPED ROCKS...

According to legend, it was the giant Gargantua who, when skipping rocks, threw these two stone blocks into the harbour from Mount Salève. *Niton* is supposedly a corruption of *Neith*, the god of the Gauls, or the Roman god Neptune. These two rocks apparently played a ritual and spiritual role. This hypothesis is based on the presence of a square-shaped hole on top of the large stone and the discovery, in 1660, of two axes and knives from the middle Bronze Age (1500-1200 BC). For scientists, the Pierres du Niton are rocks left by the Rhône glacier during the last Ice Age.

THE PEACOCK HOUSE
AND THE HOUSE OF PAN

7 and 8, avenue Pictet-de-Rochement
• Trams 12, 16, 17, Villereuse stop

> *Why do
> peacocks
> and the god Pan
> face one another?*

They stand facing one another on avenue Pictet-de-Rochemont in the Eaux-Vives neighbourhood: the Peacock (*paon* in French) House at number 7, and the House of Pan at number 8.

Few people know that these two buildings illustrate a mischievous pun by the architects, as this play on words refers to the corner bevelling of the two buildings, called *pans coupés* (cut-off corners).

The Peacock House is the most famous. Its ornamentation includes stone peacocks spreading their tails and preparing to scream (the curious term given to the call of this bird). The building's windows are overcrowded with plant sculptures and scrolls (photo below).

As for the House of Pan, its entrance is topped by two heads of the god Pan, with his goat horns and headdress of grapevines and bunches of grapes (photo opposite). The rest of the house is simpler.

Built simultaneously in 1902 and 1903 by architects Ami Golay and Eugène Cavalli (sculptures by Emile-Dominique Fasanino and ironwork by Alexandre Vailly), these two edifices constitute the most stunning expression of Art

Nouveau in Geneva. They remain a rather moderate example, however, as the luxurious ornamentation on the façade of number 7 exhibits a certain Calvinist restraint compared with French buildings of the same style.

Although the Peacock House has been a protected site since 1986, the stones of its façade crumble rather easily which, when combined with the urban pollution that insidiously chips away at it, causes visible deteriorations.

PAN: A GOD AT THE ORIGIN OF THE WORD "PANIC"

The god Pan, whose name means "everything", originally protected flocks, goatherds and shepherds. Deformed, hairy and monstrous with his goat hooves, he was the laughing stock of all of the Greek gods of Olympus. The god of fertility and sexuality, brutal in his desires and terrifying in his apparitions – the origin of the word "panic" – he was also a healer and the inventor of the pan flute, the famous flute composed of pieces of reed of varying lengths.

THE FAUNS OF 33-35 AVENUE DE MIREMONT ❾

• Bus 21, Crêts-de-Champel stop, Bus 3, Miremont stop

Child-eating ogres

The façades of the buildings at numbers 33 and 35, avenue de Miremont, built on the Champel plateau in 1910 by architects A. Boissonnas and E. Henssler, are decorated with strange and massive sculptures. They were created by Paul Moullet, a little-known artist who worked mainly in France on war memorials to the fallen soldiers of the 1914-1918 war (in the villages of Gorrevod – *Poilu holding a bayonet*, 1921 – and Jayat, both of which are in the Ain region).

On the first building, fauns can be seen with goat horns and hooves playing the role of Atlas, supporting the balcony. Their incisors clearly visible, they are devouring babies they take out of a basket held between their legs.

On the second building, a couple turn their backs above the entrance. The man is wearing a helmet and armour, and the woman a wimple. Here, also, two fauns with their arms crossed watch passers-by. The figure of a woman with a sad smile completes the scene.

For what reason did the owner, a certain Hoelscher, commission this fairytale imagery? The best historians of Genevan architecture have tried to answer this question, but to no avail. Perhaps it is related to personal memories or family secrets? We can see that only one of the children has escaped the ogre's basket by sliding down a rope...

One last note – a few phrases dedicated to these strange Champel houses in *L'inventaire Suisse d'Architecture (INSA), 1850-1920* (Swiss Architectural Inventory), state that these façades are haunted.

CHAMPEL: RUE BEAU-SÉJOUR WAS THE FORMER SITE OF EXECUTIONS!

At Champel, the executioner used to do his work at the top of what is now rue Beau-Séjour (this new name is rather ironic as, in French, it means "nice stay"). As Geneva's inhabitants greatly appreciated the spectacle of the executions, the square had to be enlarged several times. The most famous prisoner executed at Champel was Michel Servet, who rejected the concept of the Christian Trinity. He was burnt at the stake on 27 October 1553. Since the firewood used was wet, he agonized for hours... This act tormented the conscience of Geneva's Protestants for many years, to the point that, in 1903, they erected a stele of repentance at the site of execution. From the beginning of the 18th century, the Champel gallows were no longer used, but the sinister-looking structure continued to inspire fear and delayed the sector's urbanization.

THE MYSTERIOUS B OF BODMER MUSEUM ⑩

19, route du Guignard, Cologny
• Open Tuesday to Sunday, 2pm to 6pm
• Bus 9, 33, Croisée de Cologny stop

Martin Bodmer, ambidextrous

The magnificent row of skylights at the entrance to Bodmer Museum, in Cologny, poses an enigma: why is the capital B's symmetrical twin reversed? You will find no explanation anywhere and the friendly museum employees have stopped looking...

In fact this detail is reminiscent of a particularity of the founder, Martin Bodmer, who was ambidextrous. Tessin native and architect Mario Botta added this reference when he carried out the enlargement of the museum, completed in 2003.

These two Bs are engraved on five glazed spaces dedicated to the Bible, Homer, Dante, Shakespeare and Goethe, great themes that Martin Bodmer held dear. They are used to bring natural light into the underground exhibition spaces.

Mario Botta designed the museum by burying it between the two pre-existing villas. The showcases light up when visitors stand in front of them, bringing the precious documents out of the darkness. A magical voyage to the realm of the oldest documents.

FRANKENSTEIN WAS BORN IN COLOGNY!

In the summer of 1816, Mary Wollstonecraft Godwin, a 19-year-old English girl, arrived in Geneva with the poet Percy Shelley, 24. They were on an elopement of sorts, as Shelley was already married.

Mary thus joined her half-sister, Claire Claimont, Lord Byron's mistress, who one day decided to rent the Diodati villa in the hills of Cologny.

The weather was awful, with constant rain... To fight boredom, Byron proposed that they each write a Gothic story.

The two men quickly abandoned the project, but Mary persevered. Soon, her manuscript took on the size of a book. The hero was Frankenstein, a man who stole the essence of life and wanted to form a new being in the service of humanity. Alas! The experiment went wrong. Frankenstein

created a soulless monster, assembling different body parts taken from morgues and cemeteries. The novel was published anonymously in 1818 and was a phenomenal success. The young woman had invented the science-fiction genre, and moreover foreshadowed the work of Freud, with her hero who constantly fights between his dreams and his primal urges.

VESTIGES OF THE ROMAN AQUEDUCT SERVING GENEVA ⓫

Thônex, place de Graveson
• Trams 12, 16, 17, Graveson stop

> *Such effort for pure water!*

During repair work on rue de Genève (which leads to the Moillesulaz Customs House), workers discovered a section of the Roman aqueduct that brought water from the Voirons mountains to the city.

Before covering it up again, a section a few metres long was removed and was set back a little from the road on Place de Graveson.

This section is made up of low walls of river boulders with a vault made of blocks of hewn tuff. Its interior dimensions are 50cm wide and 80cm high.

The Romans dared not drink the water from lakes or rivers, which often served as sewers and swept away decaying carcasses. To get spring water, they didn't hesitate to construct aqueducts, which were sometimes gigantic, such as the famous Pont du Gard near Nîmes, France.

For Geneva, thanks to a donation made by Lucius Brocchus Valerius Bassus, a grand landowner and chief magistrate of the province, they built (probably in the middle of the 1st century) a pipe of about 11 kilometres long, starting at Cranves in the Voirons mountains, at an altitude of 130 metres.

The aqueduct crossed the Foron and Seymaz rivers on arches, and the water flowed into a main reservoir on Tranchées plateau. Then, another network of pipes distributed it to the various districts of the city (principal junctions at Traînant, Promenade du Pin, Eaux-Vives and La Grange villa).

Sections of this aqueduct had been noticed from 1838, but its exact path was not pieced together until 1928 (see below), thanks to the cantonal archaeologist of the time, Louis Blondel.

The barbarian invasions of the 3rd century damaged the structure, which was used and maintained less and less. Over time, the visible sections of the structure (the bridges and arches) disappeared first. Its secondary pipes, of about 60cm in diameter, were forgotten and progressively destroyed in excavation and construction work. In the 6th century, the aqueduct was already just a memory.

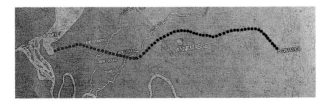

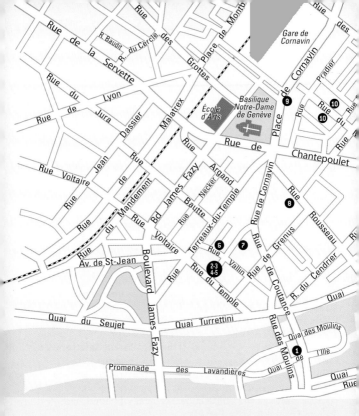

RIGHT BANK

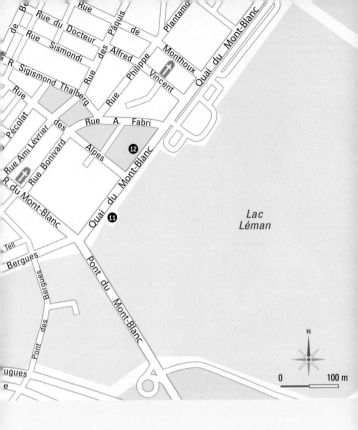

THE WEASEL ON THE STATUE OF PHILIBERT BERTHELIER

①

Tour de l'Île
• Bus 1, 5, Place Bel-Air stop

W hat is this discreet weasel doing engraved on the base of the statue of Philibert Berthelier, which stands in front of the Île Tower? This hero of Genevan history had made the animal his mascot and always carried one in his pocket. This just goes to show that the current fashion among certain marginal groups of carrying a white rat on your shoulder is nothing new!

> *"I will not die, but will live to talk about the work of the Lord"*

One of the greatest figures of Genevan history, Philibert Berthelier was, in fact, from Bresse. He was born in Virieu-le-Grand in 1465. After serving in the armies of Louis XII, he arrived in Geneva where he became one of the leaders of the "Eidguenots" faction. Unshakeable patriots, these anti-Savoyards wanted the City-State to remain independent, contrary to the ambitions of the Duke of Savoy, and to attain that goal they relied on their alliance with the Confederates. This struggle ended badly for Berthelier. In 1519, he was imprisoned by the prince-bishop John the Bastard and condemned to death. Beheaded at the exact site where his statue stands at l'Île, his body was then hung from the Champel gallows. The wait was long – nearly four centuries – for a monument to be erected in his honour. The 6 metre high statue against the Île Tower – the only vestige of the castle built around 1215 – is the work of sculptor Ampellio Regazzoni. It was inaugurated on 30 May 1909.

Berthelier is depicted with a proud posture, standing defiantly against the country's enemies. He points at a plaque upon which the phrase he wrote on the walls of his prison is engraved: "I will not die, but will live to talk about the work of the Lord."

The Château de l'Île has a complicated history. Demolished, then rebuilt only to be demolished a second time, the authorities proposed to tear down its last remaining tower in the 19th century. A popular referendum saved it in 1897... definitively?

MARKS OF FLORENTINE POWER AT SAINT GERVAIS TEMPLE

2

12, rue Terreaux-du-Temple
• Trams 15, 16, Isaac-Mercier stop
• Bus 1, Coutance stop

A reminder of the power of Florence's bankers

Although their mark on Saint Peter's is discreet, the Florentine signature is omnipresent on the stalls of Saint Gervais. The collection gathered here from several of Geneva's religious sites (primarily the Franciscan and Dominican churches) was offered during the period from 1432 to 1447. The power of the Florentine bankers was then at its height in Geneva, with representatives of the Medici family amassing fortunes and spending just as much. Their influence decreased suddenly when Louis XI, hoping to ruin the economic importance of Geneva's trade fair, decided to open rival fairs in Lyon in 1463. The Florentines followed the flow of money and left for the city on the Rhône.

The presence of the lily and coat of arms of Florence abounds in the decoration of Saint Gervais. The donors' desire to show their magnificence is very clearly asserted on the shields and banners engraved in the walnut.

Thus, the two lions supporting the coats of arms are reminiscent of the lions holding coats of arms in the Lily Room of Florence's Palazzo Vecchio.

THE RED LILY, SYMBOL OF FLORENCE

The red lily, distinctly different from that of the kings of France (which is more stylized with only the three open petals), symbolizes the city of Florence. Called the "Florentine lily", this symbol has three petals separated by stamens and more elaborate roots. It appears on the former coins of the City-State, the florin (*fiorino* linked both to *fiore* – flower – and *Fiorentia* – the old Tuscan name for the city), and gave the city its literary nickname, the City of the Red Lily.

SACRED SYMBOLISM OF THE FLEUR-DE-LIS

The fleur-de-lis is symbolically linked to the iris and the lily (*Lilium*). According to Miranda Bruce-Mitford, Louis VII the Younger (1147) was the first king of France to adopt the iris as his emblem and use it as a seal for his letters patent (decrees). Since, at the time, the name Louis was spelled *Loys*, it supposedly evolved to *"fleur-de-louis"*, then fleur-de-lis, its three petals representing Faith, Wisdom and Courage.

In reality, even if there is a strong resemblance between the iris and the fleur-de-lis, the French monarch merely adopted an ancient symbol of French heraldry. In AD 496, an angel purportedly appeared before Clotilda (wife of Clovis, king of the Francs) and offered her a lily, an event that influenced her conversion to Christianity. This miracle is also reminiscent of the story of the Virgin Mary, when the Angel Gabriel appeared to her, holding a lily, to tell her she was predestined to be the mother of the Saviour. This flower is also present in the iconography of Joseph, Mary's husband, to designate him as the patriarch of the new holy dynasty of divine royalty.

In 1125, the French flag (and coat of arms) depicted a field of fleur-de-lis. It remained unchanged until the reign of Charles V (1364), who officially adopted the symbol to honour the Holy Trinity, thus deciding to reduce the number of flowers to three. The flower's three petals also referred to the Trinity.

The lily stylized into a fleur-de-lis is also a Biblical plant associated with the emblem of King David as well as Jesus Christ ("consider the lilies of the field…" Matthew 6:28-29). It also appears in Egypt in association with the lotus flower, as well as in the Assyrian and Muslim cultures. It became an early symbol of power and sovereignty, and of the realm of Divine Law, thus also signifying the purity of the body and soul. This is why the ancient kings of Europe were divine, consecrated by the Divinity through sacerdotal authority. Thus, theoretically, they were to be fair, perfect and pure beings as the Virgin Mary had been, she who is the "Lily of the Annunciation and Submission" (*Ecce Ancila Domine*, "Here is the Servant of the Lord," as Luke the Apostle reveals), and the holy patron of all royal power.

The lily thus replaced the iris, which explains why, in Spanish, "fleur-de-lis" becomes *"flor del lírio"*, and why the two flowers are symbolically associated with the same lily.

Botanically, the fleur-de-lis is neither an iris nor a lily. The iris (*Iris germanica*) is a plant of the Iridaceae family that originates in northern Europe. The more commonly known lily species (*Lilium pumilum*, *Lilium speciosum*, *Lilium candidum*) are members of the Liliaceae family that originates in Central Asia and Asia Minor. The true fleur-de-lis belongs to neither the Iridaceae nor the Liliaceae family. It is the *Sprekelia formosissima*, a member of the Amaryllidaceae family that originates in Mexico and Guatemala. Known in other languages as the Aztec lily, the São Tiago lily, and the St James lily, *Sprekelia formosissima* is the only species of the genus. It was named in the 18th century by botanist Carl von Linné when he received a few bulbs from J.H. Van Sprekelsen, a German lawyer. The Spanish introduced the plant to Europe when they brought bulbs back from Mexico at the end of the 16th century.

The monarchs and princes of Portugal knew of its symbolic meaning much earlier, however, since, roughly from the time of Afonso Henriques, and especially from the late 13th century, the lily, converted or stylized into the fleur-de-lis, appeared prominently on Portuguese coats of arms, with all its inherent, immediate and essential symbolism. This was due to the Arab influence that brought it from Egypt to the Iberian Peninsula during the occupation.

𝔓our bié

MISERICORDS OF SAINT GERVAIS TEMPLE

12, rue Terreaux-du-Temple
• Trams 15, 16, Isaac-Mercier stop
• Bus 1, Coutance stop
• Mass every Sunday at 10am
• E-mail: contact@espace-saint-gervais.ch

*Colourful
symbols*

The work of unknown artisans,* twelve misericords have survived on the stalls of Saint Gervais. The most surprising one, which was probably located on the fourth of the high stalls in the northern row (now occupied by a modern, undecorated console), is no longer present. This misericord depicted an acrobat, called "exhibitionist", because he exposed his genitals in a provocative contortion. The sculpture was given to the Museum of Art and History in 1891. The character's face and intimate parts had been mutilated.

The first misericord of in this row depicts a fool playing bagpipes and wearing a cap with donkey ears; a bell hangs between his legs. This is undoubtedly a reference to the clergy's famous saturnalia, a feast for idiots that sub-deacons greatly enjoyed in the Middle Ages.

The second misericord shows a mermaid with a cleft tail. Her right arm, which held a mirror, has been broken and her left arm combs her long hair. Combs and mirrors were the symbols of lust and prostitution.

The third misericord of the high stalls in the southern row represents a nanny and a billy goat face-to-face, which is another traditional image of lust.

The third misericord of the low stalls shows two opposed faces united under the same hood. It is meant to illustrate the passing of time, with the old face symbolizing the past year, and the young one turned towards the new year.

The fourth misericord depicts a glutton with his head stuck in a cauldron, symbol of the punishment for the sin of gluttony.

*In her thesis "Sculpted stalls from the 15th century" (from which most of the above information is taken), historian Corinne Charles provides a long list of the artisans who worked in Geneva at the time. The creators of these little marvels are probably among them.

SAINT GERVAIS ARCHAEOLOGICAL SITE

Saint Gervais Temple
12, rue des Terreaux-du-Temple
• Trams 14, 15, 16, Isaac-Mercier stop
• Tours upon request at the Service Cantonal d'Archéologie
• Tel: +41 (0)22 327 24 86
• E-mail: scag@etat.ge.ch

6,000 years of history finally revealed

Although the archaeological site beneath Saint Peter's Cathedral is well-known and popular with visitors, the one beneath Saint Gervais Temple has only been open to the public since the summer of 2009, and only upon request at the Service Cantonal d'Archéologie (Cantonal Department of Archaeology). Curious Genevans are thus just discovering this site.

Before, little was known about what once existed on the other side of the bridge that Julius Caesar destroyed in 58 BC (to keep the Helvetians from crossing via the left bank). The excavations under Saint Gervais allowed archaeologists to trace back through history.

The first recorded settlement thus dates from the Middle Neolithic Period (4000 BC). This hill overlooking the Rhône also served as a burial site in the Late Bronze Age (1000 BC), and was then the site of stone alignments (Iron Age, around 800 BC).

Around AD 500, a first church was built to shelter the tomb of an important figure, perhaps one of the first bishops of Geneva, beneath its elevated choir in a tomb that served as a crypt.

The walls of the cross-shaped early Christian church have been preserved and constitute the exterior of the site's central section. Access to the crypt, through lateral passages added in the 15th century, also lets visitors discover the annexes placed on both sides of the choir. One of them, endowed with an apse, dates from the 6th century and houses monumental tombs. In this period, and in the 7th century, numerous sepulchres formed by molasse slabs stood in the areas below and around the church. Around the nave, a visible portico protects them and the Gallo-Roman sanctuary beneath the esplanade north of the temple.

PLAQUE OF THE GENEVAN HEROES ❺

12, rue Terreaux-du-Temple
• Trams 15, 16, Isaac-Mercier stop
• Bus 1, Coutance stop

> *The little-known list of the 14 Savoyards tortured in the Escalade*

The Genevans know everything about the Escalade of 1602 in which their ancestors repelled the Savoyard attack, yet they generally admit their ignorance when asked about the list of the thirteen – the commonly given number – Savoyard prisoners that were hung and beheaded at 2:30pm the day after the attack, on 12 December. The most informed can only give two or three of the more famous names... Reading the works of eminent historians does not help much either. Rather than remembering their enemies, the Genevans prefer to honour the seventeen heroes who fell in this battle. On the wall of Saint Gervais Temple, along rue des Corps-Saints, there is a marble plaque bearing their names: Jean Canal, Jean Vandel, Louis Bandière, Nicolas Bogueret, Pierre Cabriol, Michel Monnard, Jean Guignet, Marc Cambiago, Daniel Humbert, Louis Gallatin, Abraham de Baptista, Jean-Jacques Mercier, Philippe Poteau, Martin de Bolo, Jacques Petit, François Bousezel, and Gérard Musy. A final name to add to the list is that of Jacques Billon, who died from his wounds a few days later.

Why is this plaque located so far away from the Old City and where the attack took place? Because the

valiant dead were buried in the cemetery that used to stand next to the temple. When the cemetery was removed in 1774, the commemorative plaque was simply moved a few metres away. In 1603, the pastors suggested to the Council that it would be more judicious to put this monument at the Treille, but the request was rejected. Perhaps this error will be corrected one day.

THE 14 SAVOYARDS HUNG AND BEHEADED AFTER THE ESCALADE

Since the Registers of the Dead covering the period from 1600 to 1608 have disappeared from the Cantonal Archives, we can only rely on the writings of those who had the opportunity to consult them before the theft. A text by Alex Guillot (1915) notes that, according to the Register of the Council of Geneva dating from the notorious day of 12 December 1602 (Julian calendar), there were fourteen prisoners, not thirteen! Here is the list, in the same order and names with the same spelling as in the document:

1. Jacques, son of Charles Chafardon, from Saint-Jean d'Arbey, near Chambéry.
2. François, son of the late Ayme de Gerbel, lord of Sonna.
3. Pierre, son of Philibert de Montluçon, lord of Attignac, in Bresse.
4. Donat, son of François Payant, from Trez in Provence.
5. Soupfre, son of Bonaventure Galiffet, from Saint-Laurent, near the Echelles.
6. Anthoine, son of Laurent de Concière, from Angrelat in Dauphiné.
7. Philibert, son of Laurent Sadou, from Tagninge.
8. Pierre Vulliens, from Bourg.
9. Jaques Durand, from Nevers.
10. Jean Clerc, from Migeveta.
11. Jacques Bovier, alias corporal La Lime, from Seyssel.
12. Pierre Mathieu, from Usez, carder.
13. Jean de Banardi, from Talars in Dauphiné.
14. Jacques Bouzonnet.

Some of the prisoners – the lord of Gruffy? – may not have given their true name. Beheaded after their hanging, their bodies were thrown into the Rhône and their heads exposed on pikes for six months. Only the body of the Count of Sonnaz was returned to his wife, Louise d'Alby.

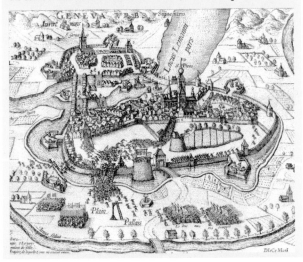

THE BAS-RELIEF OF RUE VALLIN

Rue Vallin
• Trams 14, 15, 16, Isaac-Mercier stop
• Bus 1, Coutance stop

> *A souvenir of the "fabrique" of Saint Gervais*

The large bas-relief (5.62m x 2.6m) on a façade at the corner of rue Vallin and place Simon-Goulart, entitled *L'ATELIER*, is a reminder of how this district was once inhabited by artisans of all sorts. Inaugurated in 1958, it is the work of sculptor Paul Bianchi (a Graubünden, born in 1920 at Coire and died at Carouge in 1973) and depicts a master with his apprentice.

The *cabinotiers* (see below) particularly built the reputation of Saint Gervais as a crowded, rebellious district, in contrast to the well-off, conservative Geneva of the left bank. Around 1800, the clockmakers and their trade, nicknamed the "*fabrique*" (factory), provided a living for the 5,000 to 26,000 inhabitants living in Geneva at the time. This population was packed in a maze of alleys and increasingly rickety buildings that were a delight for amateur watercolourists but a nightmare for the people who lived there.

From 1895 to 1901, the construction of rue Vallin made way for "hygienic" buildings financed by the savings bank. Although the sought-after goal was to improve the living conditions of these blocks of misery, the destruction was a bit too systematic and many precious emblems of the past were also lost. The construction work of this zone running all the way down to the Rhône accelerated around 1930 – in 1929, 800 foreign workers were "invited" to leave the canton – and period photos show enormous gaps and vast expanses of rubble.

WHERE DOES THE WORD *CABINOTIER* COME FROM?

The clockmakers of Saint Gervais worked on the upper floors, where they received the most light. These little workshops were called "*cabinets*", hence the term *cabinotiers*.

SIGHTS NEARBY

AU VIEUX ST-GERVAIS BOUTIQUE

At 10, rue des Corps-Saints, in the *Au Vieux St-Gervais*, Bruno Pesenti, an old watch enthusiast, occupies a minuscule arch in which he indulges his passion for the restoration and collection of antique pieces, as a worthy successor of the Genevan *cabinotiers*. His workshop-boutique is a veritable museum of its own.

THE SECRET PASSAGES OF SAINT GERVAIS

In the Saint Gervais district, once crammed with the *cabinotiers'* (artisan clockmakers) workshops, an entire network of passages and shortcuts connecting courtyards and buildings is now out of bounds to the public. Politicians dream of reopening these secret barriers, knocking down locked gates, and penetrating once again these interior courtyards.

At least four have been counted. The first connects number 18, rue de Coutance to number 9, place De-Grenus. At its centre is a remarkable inner courtyard and tower, the vestige of the 15th-century fortifications. Looking closely, you can see a loophole from which defenders riddled their enemies with arrows. On the other side is a Florentine-style building with colonnades.

The second shortcut links number 6, place De-Grenus to number 9, rue Rousseau. The interior courtyard has been tastefully renovated, and the monumental flight of steps opens onto beautiful arches ornamented with wrought-iron guardrails on each floor.

The third passage, between rue Lissignol and rue Rousseau (number 14), also includes a 19th-century inner courtyard, but no historic elements have been preserved. The fourth shortcut begins at number 10, rue Lissignol and ends at number 9, rue de Chantepoulet. So in just a short distance you go from very modest and calm dwellings, on the Lissignol side, to the noisy and busy thoroughfare of Chantepoulet. At the centre of this passage, the only luxury is the inner courtyard: a tree twists its branches all the way up towards the blue sky...

Will these shortcuts, many of which merit a historically respectful restoration, be reopened to the public one day? The owners fear for their safety, but why not leave them open during the day, or during certain events such as the Heritage Days?

ROUSSEAU'S FALSE BIRTHPLACE ⑧

27, rue Jean-Jacques Rousseau
• Bus 1, 3, 19, Coutance stop

> **When it was believed Jean-Jacques Rousseau was born in Saint Gervais**

At the first-floor level of the building at 27, rue Jean-Jacques Rousseau, an almost illegible plaque damaged by pollution states: "In 1793, the Genevan authorities renamed rue Chevelu after Jean-Jacques Rousseau."

In fact, this inscription corrects a monumental error. In 1793, it was believed that Jean-Jacques Rousseau was born here, in the Saint Gervais district where he lived during his adolescence. A grandiose ceremony, with a parade, patriotic speeches and the placement of a commemorative plaque, took place at this very spot.

The authorities, ashamed, later had to admit that it was all false, even if the error was not officially recognized until 1904 and the original plaque replaced with this corrected inscription. Rue Chevelu (named after a noteworthy figure probably from the 16th century) was renamed at this time and justly became rue Jean-Jacques Rousseau.

We know that the writer was actually born at number 40, Grand-Rue, in the Old City, on 28 June 1712. His mother died a few days later, on 7 July, of puerperal fever, which killed so many women at the time.

His father, of modest means, made him an apprentice to a Saint Gervais clockmaker. One night, the young rascal found himself forced to spend the night outside the city walls for the third time (he had missed the closing of the gates), so he chose to run away definitively to France.

In 1754, now famous, he came back to spend a few months in Geneva. Back in France, he was welcomed at the home of Madame d'Epinay at Montmorency, where he wrote *La Nouvelle Héloïse* (1761), the *Social Contract* and *Emile* (1762). These two later works, in particular, enraged the powers that

be, including those of Geneva. The books were publically burned in front of the town hall and the philosopher was condemned to exile.

Outraged, Rousseau resolved to renounce his Genevan citizenship in 1763. Fleeing across Europe, and often destitute, he died in 1778 in Ermenonville (Oise, France), at the home of the Marquis de Girardin, who had taken him in. Worn-out and old before his time, he was 66.

Towards the end of his life, Rousseau strangely dressed as an Armenian, with a fur hat, coat, dolman and belt.

THE REVENGE OF A SHUNNED STATUE

Even if Geneva has patched things up with Jean-Jacques Rousseau today, to the point of dedicating a "Space" to him in his place of birth at 40, Grand-Rue (see opposite), their relations were much cooler during his lifetime. When the Council condemned him to exile in 1762, Rousseau replied by renouncing "in perpetuity to my right of bourgeoisie and to be established in the City and Republic of Geneva" (letter to the mayor on 12 May 1763).

Furthermore, when a committee launched the idea of erecting a statue of the philosopher in 1828 to celebrate the 50th anniversary of his death, the Council half-heartedly agreed to help finance it. A statue was nevertheless commissioned from sought-after artist James Pradier. When the work arrived from Paris, the conservative government's reluctance was far from forgotten. Where could this monumental statue be placed without seeming to approve the principles of a man formerly accused of "aiming to destroy the Christian religion and all governments"?

A compromise was found. This Rousseau, seated and in Roman dress, was placed well away from the centre on the island that was then called Île des Barques (Boat Island), and facing the Bergues Bridge. Was the philosopher's regard still too troublesome? In 1850, it was hidden behind three rows of poplar trees.

Finally, in 1862, it was turned around towards the lake... the Mont-Blanc bridge was about to be inaugurated.

ROOM "122" OF THE CORNAVIN HOTEL ⑨

Place Gare de Cornavin
33, boulevard James-Fazy

> *Professor Calculus' room!*

The Cornavin Hotel has almost known global fame ever since Hergé had the heroes of Tintin stay there in *The Calculus Affair*. When the comic-strip album was published in 1956, the cartoonist returned to the site where he did his first location-hunting and spent two nights at the hotel in room 210.

Tintin fans who have flocked here from all over the world prefer to remember room 122, however, as this is where Professor Calculus is meant to have stayed.

A surprising fact, this room didn't originally exist and was simply the fruit of

Hergé's imagination. Forty-two years later, faced with insistent clients, the hotel finally added one when the establishment was renovated in 1998.

Visitors staying in this room often try to "forget" to return the key when they leave, so the employees at the reception desk – where a statue of Tintin with his mop of red hair stands imposingly near the entrance – are particularly vigilant.

To draw the embassy of Borduria, where some of the action of *The Calculus Affair* takes place, Hergé was inspired in part by the building of the Hotel Management School of Geneva.

The Cornavin Hotel possesses the highest pendulum clock in the world, standing 30.02m tall! The work of Swiss native Jean Kazès, it is listed in the *Guinness Book of World Records*.

THE FORGOTTEN PEREGRINATIONS ❿
OF THE FORMER RUSSIAN HOTEL'S SPHINXES

26, rue du Mont-Blanc
Pedestrian area
• Bus 8, Chantepoulet stop

Guardians
of rue
du Mont-Blanc

The pink marble sphinxes with curvaceous breasts at 26, rue du Mont-Blanc, spent many years guarding the entrance to the Russian Hotel, which once stood at the other end of the street at the corner of Quai du Mont-Blanc, across from the bridge. This hotel was the result of the conversion of the beautiful residence of James Fazy, the father of the Constitution of 1847, who died bankrupt. The State had awarded him this plot of land in recognition of his political contributions.

The Russian Hotel was demolished in the 1960s, to the great regret of Genevans, to make way for a commercial building. The two sphinxes were thus sold at auction. Purchased by the owner of a campsite in the canton of Vaud, at Avenches – for just 3,500 Swiss francs – they were forgotten for a few years. When the city wanted to decorate the upper part of rue du Mont-Blanc, near Cornavin railway station, they remembered the great presence of these sphinxes that formed part of Geneva's collective memory. The authorities rediscovered them in 1982 and acquired them for 8,000 francs.

Today, they guard either side of the pedestrian street, thus at the opposite end from their original home. They date from 1855 and are the work of François Lempereur, born in Rupt (Haute-Saône, France).

WHERE DOES THE NAME "CORNAVIN" COME FROM?

Centuries before the station and street took this name, Cornavin was a locality.

A corruption of the term *corne à vin* (wine horn), Cornavin refers to the grapevines that, until the beginning of the 15th century, provided the bishops with more than enough wine for Mass.

According to some historians, an inn called *"La Corne à vin"* was located outside the city walls, at this site, which is what gave the district its name.

A few acres of vines survived on the hill to a later date, which permitted Voltaire to appreciate their flavour with enthusiasm: "This wine is of singular and admirable quality"!

THE BLOODSTAINED ROSE AND RIBBON OF SISSI THE EMPRESS

⑪

Beau-Rivage Hotel
13, quai du Mont-Blanc
• Bus 6, 8, 9, 27, Mont-Blanc stop

T he Beau-Rivage Hotel (13, quai du Mont-Blanc) holds a moving reminder of Sissi's assassination in 1898. In a glass frame kept on the first floor, you can see a rose and ribbon stained with her imperial blood.

> *Assassinated by the anarchist Lucheni*

On 10 September 1898, the Empress of Austria and Queen of Hungary, affectionately known as "Sissi", left the Beau-Rivage Hotel accompanied by her lady-in-waiting, Countess Sztaray. The two women headed towards the Mont-Blanc pier, where the ship "Genève" was awaiting them, at 1:40pm, for a lake cruise to Territet.

Halfway there, opposite the Hotel de la Paix and the bottom of rue des Alpes, a 25-year-old Italian anarchist, Luigi Lucheni, suddenly appeared and stabbed the empress with a long, sharp blade. Believing she had only received a violent blow to the chest, Sissi boarded the "Genève" while the authorities chased her attacker. But her dress became stained with blood In fact, the blade had gone straight through her left ventricle and lung.

Taken back to the Beau-Rivage on a stretcher, the empress died at 2:10pm. She was 61 years old.

Although the sparkle of her youth was immortalized on film by Romy Schneider, some details of the end of her life are less well known. For example, she wore dentures and used raw meat face masks to keep her complexion. Her assassin was condemned to life in prison, but he hung himself in his cell twelve years later.

THE ASSASSIN'S HEAD PRESERVED IN VIENNA

A morbid detail: Lucheni's head was preserved in a jar of formaldehyde and, after a number of adventures, was finally sent to Vienna, where it remains today.

Near the Beau-Rivage Hotel, Sissi's assassination is remembered in several places. A plaque attached to a guardrail on Quai du Mont-Blanc marks the exact site of the attack. On a nearby lawn, an association to the memory of the Empress of Austria had a statue of the empress holding a fan erected in 1998 for the 100th anniversary of her death.

THE ROVING STATUE
OF THE DUKE OF BRUNSWICK

⑫

Square des Alpes, Quai du Mont-Blanc
• Bus 1, Navigation stop

*A statue
that was
originally on top
of a mausoleum*

Hoping that one of the most powerful European monarchs (Emperor Napoleon III, the King of Prussia, or even Tsar Alexander II) would finally recognize his rights as heir and oblige his brother and the King of Hanover to return the German possessions they had "stolen" from him, the Duke of Brunswick made a provisional will in favour of Geneva.

But, in 1873, death took the duke and a tidy sum fell into the city's coffers: almost a billion Swiss francs in today's money!

One of the conditions of receiving the fabulous fortune was to build a mausoleum according to the duke's wishes and plans in an "eminent and dignified" spot. The established project was a copy, enlarged by one-fifth, of the Scaligeri family tomb in Verona. The Genevans accepted, of course. The duke's monument, completed by the best artists of the period, was erected near the lake and inaugurated in 1879. It cost slightly less than 10% of the inheritance.

The rest was used to embellish and transform the city, as well as to build several prestigious monuments, such as the Grand Théâtre.

Respecting the wishes of this heir to the dukedom of Brunswick-Wolfenbüttel, who was chased off his lands by his aristocracy in 1830 (when he was 26), the equestrian statue was initially placed at the top of the mausoleum. However, it was soon noted that the statue was too heavy and risked falling with every blast of the North wind. After four nerve-wracking years, it was taken down in 1883 and set in a corner of the square des Alpes.

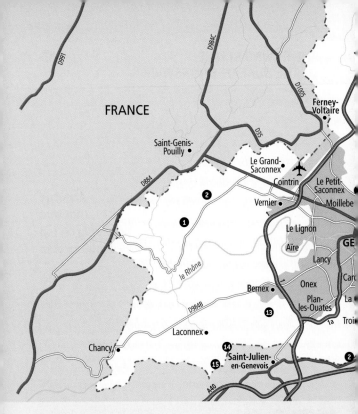

CANTON

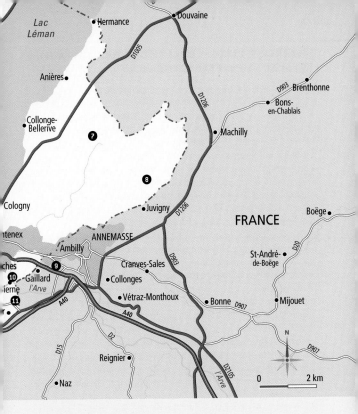

THE CHÂTEAU OF DARDAGNY AND *LE CAPITAINE FRACASSE*: WHAT IS THE TRUE DÉCOR DESCRIBED BY THÉOPHILE GAUTIER?

Access: Train 96744, La Plaine stop, then Bus X to Dardagny

At the beginning of *Le Capitaine Fracasse*, Théophile Gautier describes at length the *château de la Misère* (misery), the rundown property of his hero, the Baron of Sigognac. Did he use the château of Dardagny as a model? This is the most commonly held hypothesis.

However, if Dardagny manor did, in fact, inspire Théophile Gautier, then it was rather to describe a second château appearing much later in the novel – the château of Bruyères, which, in the book, belongs to a rich marquis.

Indeed, a close reading of the text supports this interpretation. Théophile Gautier described the château of Bruyères as follows:

Four rustic coupled columns, their bases alternately round and square, supported a cornice emblazoned with the marquis' coat of arms that formed the platform of a large balcony with a stone balustrade, above which opened the lounge's master window... The window frames were cut in beautiful white stone and the lintels in the same material accentuated the separation between the floors...

These elements are almost the same as those of the château of Dardagny's façade (photo below). And even if Théophile Gautier then embellished it – he writes of three storeys whereas there are only two, and he adds details not found here – the comparison between the two manors described in *Le Capitaine Fracasse* clearly tips the scales: the château of Dardagny is not the miserable *château de la Misère*, but certainly the sumptuous château de Bruyères

For the benefit of sceptics, we should also note that, in the novel,

the *château de la Misère* has only twelve windows on its façade and two round towers, whereas Dardagny has thirty-two windows and square towers. Of course, accuracy was not likely to be Théophile Gautier's main worry, and he probably combined descriptions of several manors to recount the exploits of Captain Fracasse.

Théophile Gautier made numerous extended trips to Geneva to visit his mistress, Carlotta Grisi, an Italian dancer married to Jules Perrot. He married her sister, Ernestine, so he wouldn't be separated from Carlotta. Carlotta Grisi's villa, in the Saint Jean neighbourhood, no longer exists, although her grave is in Châtelaine cemetery.

THE REASON FOR THE CHURCH OF PEISSY'S ❶ ISOLATED FAÇADE

Train R 96712 and bus W, Peissy stop
• Bus 67, Peissy stop

I n Peissy, only the façade of the small medieval church of Saint Paul still remains. The front entrance, topped by a bell tower, is walled up. A garden at the rear is the reminder of a surprising village quarrel.

Remnants of an old quarrel

Mentioned for the first time in 1295, even if it is probably older, the church was deconsecrated before the Revolution. In the 19th century, historian James Galiffe wanted to enlarge his property,

but the church hindered his plans. Thus, in 1826, he asked the village for authorization to pull it down. This marked the beginning of four years of unforgettable disputes and heated negotiations. Finally, a compromise was found: Galiffe could demolish the chapel, said to be a hideout for prowlers, but he had to keep the façade facing the street. The yoke – the piece of wood supporting the bell – was turned around so that the bell could be used as a fire alarm.

The façade's belltower-arch with a single opening is characteristic of the first regional churches, which justified its listing as a historic monument in 1933.

THE LAST GENEVAN *CAPITES*

Bourdigny
• Bus 67, Bourdigny-Dessus stop
Croix-de-Rozon, chemin de Verbant
Bus 46, Saconnex-Arve-Dessus stop

> **Witnesses
> to manual labour
> in the vineyards**

In the past, *capites* (vintner's huts) were built in the centre of large Genevan vineyards when the villages were too far away. They served as a place for those working the vines to eat and find shelter from the weather. A table, four chairs, and a straw mattress were the essential furnishings. Materials and tools were also stocked there. Some *capites* were veritable little one-storey houses, overlooking an ocean of grapevines. These witnesses of a time when the vines could only be maintained through manual labour are sometimes remarkable. Some have even been listed as historic monuments, including the one on chemin de

Vebant, in the village of Bardonnex (La Croix-de-Rozon). Its four-sided roof with two supporting posts and its molasse window frames are exceptional. It bears the date 1773 (photo opposite).

However the most beautiful, also built in the 18th century, stands in the vineyard of Bourdigny. It's like a doll's house with its sea-green balcony and shutters. Visitors don't get too close out of respect for the vineyards and content themselves by admiring and photographing it from afar (photo this page).

These vintner's huts were common in most wine-making regions. They are called *capite* in the area around Lake Geneva, and *guérite* in the Valais region, *cabotte* in Burgundy, *cabole* in the Beaujolais region and *ciabotta* in Liguria.

There are also numerous *capitelles* in the region around Nîmes, France, built in drystone, where they served as cabins for the small vineyards won from the scrubland in the 18th and 19th centuries.

THE "PETRIFIED" IN FRONT OF PALAIS WILSON

3

Palais Wilson
Quai Wilson
• Bus 1, Navigation stop

> **Symbols of individual destiny and solidarity between nations**

On the terrace of the Palais Wilson cafeteria, behind the gates that keep the public out but also reinforce the allegory, a group of eight kneeling "petrified" people are frozen in silent stone. Entitled *Signe d'espoir* (Sign of Hope), this work, according to Swiss artist Carl Bucher, represents the archetypes of the human race. Taken individually, they represent the destiny of everyman and everywoman. As a group, they represent nations, nations standing by one another, which protect the weakest and try to break their own chains through justice. Here, we find the essence of human rights…

Switzerland gave the work to the UN Office of the High Commissioner for Human Rights on 19 June 2006. Another group of "petrified" people can be found at the entrance to the International Museum of the Red Cross and Red Crescent, 17, avenue de la Paix.

PALAIS WILSON: AN EVENTFUL EXISTENCE

Before housing the UN Office of the High Commissioner for Human Rights, Palais Wilson had an eventful past. Inaugurated in 1875, it was first of all the most prestigious palace in Geneva. Then, at the expense of Paris and Brussels which were also in the running, it became the headquarters of the League of Nations, in 1919, under the influence of American President Woodrow Wilson. As the LON found this constantly renovated and converted building to be too cramped, it finally moved into the current Palais des Nations in 1936.

Two fires ravaged Palais Wilson, in 1985 and 1987. It was at this time that its ongoing use was put into question: what could be done with this immense, empty shell next to the lake? In 1990, the Genevans voted and decided that the city should return to its original project – a luxury hotel and convention centre. But funds were lacking…

The Federal Council took over in 1994 and the Chambers voted to approve a loan of 75 million francs to restore the building. Meant to house an "Environment Centre", Palais Wilson ultimately welcomed the Office of the High Commissioner for Human Rights in 1998.

MON-REPOS VILLA

120, rue de Lausanne
• Bus 1, Sécheron stop

> *Casanova's erotic lakeside frolics*

The individual who left the most licentious memory at Mon-Repos Villa was certainly Casanova, the adventurer with ten trades and 122 conquests. During his third visit to Geneva in 1762 (he was 37), the Italian libertine got his banker Robert Tronchin to lend him the villa. In his work *Histoire de ma vie* (Story of my Life), he tells of an evening he spent with two young and very wild Genevan

girls, Hélène and Edwige, providing spicy details of their lovemaking, which continued in the garden, near the pond.

The Mon-Repos property, bequeathed to the city in 1898, became the first public park on Lake Geneva. Before, the elegant villa, built here in 1848, had seen its share of famous guests pass through its doors, notably the Danish author Hans Christian Andersen. (At Collonges-Bellerive, across the lake, the statue of a "Little Mermaid", the heroine of one of his stories, basks on a rock. The main attraction of "Nymph" beach, she is the work of sculptor De Senger.)

After having housed the Museum of Ethnography and the Experimental Television Centre, the villa is now the headquarters of the Henry Dunant Centre for Humanitarian Dialogue (under renovation). A small stone pavilion built next to the lake houses the limnology station (the study of the physical and biological phenomena of lakes), established by Philippe Plantamour in 1877.

THE FORGOTTEN PEREGRINATIONS OF A PACIFIST WORK

❺

Place des Nations
• Trams 13, 15, Bus 8, Place des Nations stop

> *How the Cannon of Peace escaped becoming scrap metal...*

Although the *Cannon of Peace* is a powerful symbol, set back in the square in front of the Palais des Nations, it nevertheless almost ended up as scrap metal.

Created by artist Brandenberger from the canton of Glarus, the *Cannon of Peace* was installed on the Palais Wilson esplanade in October 1983, on which occasion a march had been organized to transport the work to Geneva. The participants thus wanted to encourage the Disarmament Conference to continue its work. Their hopes were soon dashed, however, as the talks were suspended a month later.

In 1994, when the Palais Wilson esplanade's underground parking lot was built, the sculpture – entitled *Frieden* ("peace" in German) – was stored in a

warehouse. In 2001, a group of citizens, concerned about this prolonged absence, launched a petition requesting that the *Cannon of Peace* be included in the plans for upgrading Place des Nations, which were under discussion at the time.

That's how this cannon, the end of which is knotted and from which hangs the wheel of a locomotive (according to the artist, this circular form represents absolute perfection), found its place near the curved building of the World Intellectual Property Organization (WIPO).

THE SURPRISING HISTORY ❻
OF THE JAPANESE BELL IN ARIANA GARDENS

Jardins de l'Ariana
• Bus 1, 5, 8, 11, Palais des Nations/Avenue de la Paix stop

The extraordinary history of the Japanese bell that now stands imposingly in Ariana park began with a stunning discovery in the Rüetschi foundries in Aarau by the great collector and patron of the arts Gustave Revilliod at the end of the 19th century. What circumstances led this magnificent one-ton Japanese bell to end up here in the Swiss canton of Aargau? Revilliod (1817-1890) made no attempt to solve the mystery when he bought the bell and placed it near his Ariana museum.

A bell that was found, returned, and then given away!

Years later, Japanese diplomats visiting Geneva recognized the bell. It was indeed the one that had graced Honsen-ji temple in Shinagawa, a Tokyo suburb. This bronze bell, cast in 1657, had disappeared after a fire at the temple in 1867. It was impossible to be mistaken, as the bell bears the names of the first three shoguns (generals) and avatars of Kan'non (the bodhisattva Avalokiteshvara, venerated under different names in the East by Buddhists). It was the fourth shogun – Tokugawa Yoshinobu – of the Tokugawa dynasty who gave this bell to the temple. This dynasty reigned from 1603 to 1867, when regime change led to the disastrous turmoil at Honsen-ji temple.

In a praiseworthy gesture, Switzerland returned the bell in 1910, but eighty years later, this good deed was rewarded: Junna Nakada, the son of the man who had negotiated the original bell's return to Japan, offered Geneva a replica. In 1991, the replica was thus suspended beneath a solidly-supported shelter in Ariana gardens.

A UN FRESCO CREATED BY A CENTENARIAN PAINTER

The fresco that brightens up the entrance to the UN, place des Nations, is undoubtedly the only one of its kind in the world. Its creator, Hans Herni, was over 100 years old when it was unveiled in June 2009. To celebrate the event, fifty-six other Genevan centenarians were invited. The centenarian artist, who was in brilliant form, explained his work: "I did my best to make this fresco as transparent as possible, in order to give the illusion of breaking through the walls of this UN, a marvellous non-belligerent organization!"

CHÂTEAU DE ROUELBEAU EXCAVATION SITE ❼

- Bus A, Carre-d'Amont stop

> *The castle of the White Lady has not yet revealed all its secrets*

The ruins of Rouelbeau castle have long been surrounded in mystery and legend, like that of the White Lady, who is said to reappear at the stroke of midnight every year at Christmas, or that of the Black Cat that you must ruthlessly knock senseless if you don't want to find yourself in hell…

The archaeologists who opened their vast excavation site in 2001 have revealed more specific discoveries, however: pieces of crossbows and pottery, a ceramic hunting horn, and, above all, a metal seal bearing the effigy of Innocent IV, who was pope from 1243 to 1254. It sealed a Papal bull authorizing Aymon II of Faucigny, owner of Rouelbeau's lands, to establish chapels in the fortified villages of Monthoux and Hermance. Listed as a historic monument since 1921, the Rouelbeau ruins are a rare example of a castle built on a plain. Originally built in wood, the castle was demolished by the forces of Bern in 1536, and then used as a source of dressed stone to build neighbouring farms. Fortunately, this bad habit is no longer followed today. The archaeologists dig as excavations are organized, and a restoration of some parts of the castle has even been considered. It is likely that their work will put an end to a local legend that tells of a tunnel through which the castle's residents could flee in case of siege. In such marshy ground, the existence of an underground tunnel seems highly unlikely…

THE LEGEND OF THE WHITE LADY

The White Lady had a bad reputation. Foolhardy individuals who risked visiting the castle ruins on Christmas night never returned… Once, however, a poor peasant decided to go hunting for wild game, hoping to offer his old mother a Christmas dinner. At the stroke of midnight, the White Lady suddenly appeared. The peasant pleaded his case with so much conviction that the ghost yielded: "*For you, I'm going to make an exception… Follow me.*" At that instant, the castle was transformed from a pile of rocks to reappear in all its former glory, brightly lit, decorated and resounding with song and joy. The White Lady took the peasant to the cellars and told him to take whatever he wanted from the chests overflowing with treasure. He avidly filled his hunting bag, his boots and his cap with gold coins. He returned to the castle courtyard as the echo of the last stroke of midnight faded. Suddenly, he found himself in the dark, surrounded by crumbling walls. But the gold hadn't disappeared as he could feel its weight in his pockets! He became the wealthiest man in the land. As for the White Lady, no one ever saw her again. Except perhaps for those who never returned to tell the tale…

THE WALLS OF THE WEAVER'S FARMHOUSE ⑧

27, route du Château-l'Évêque
Jussy
• Bus 27 or C, Jussy-Place stop

Walls
of a farm built
with historic
boundary
markers

Dozens of stone boundary markers have been removed over time. What has become of these historic objects bearing the G of Geneva, the S of Sardinia, dates, escutcheons and coats of arms? They can be found just about everywhere, on both sides of the border. Thus, the marker stone that is now planted in the lawn of the French sub-prefecture of Saint-Julien (BF 78A), or the four aligned in front of the Commanderie (stronghouse) of Compesières (BF 77A, 69 bis, 79, 71), all originate from the realignment of route nationale 206.

Many others are scattered throughout the canton and have essentially become decorative elements. The office of the Genevan Land Registry owns two, the largest of which (70 bis) comes from the crossroads at Archamps (Landecy).

In one case, however, they were reused as construction materials. These beautiful white dressed stones were thus used to frame doors and windows

when the weaver's farmhouse at 27, route du Château-l'Évêque in Jussy was built.

On further examination, twenty such stones were counted in the house, all probably dating from the 1749 and 1754 treaties, called "the boundaries", signed with the kingdom of Sardinia and France, boundaries which were rendered null and void by the redrawing of new borders in 1815. An entire page of history is thus contained in the walls of a farm, with embedded upside-down G and S, and engraved numbers that could lead to more interesting research…

HOUSE OF THE HEROIC IRÈNE GUBIER ❾

Gaillard, *douane* of Moillesulaz
• Trams 12, 16, 17, Moillesulaz stop

A passing point for Jews

Two steps from the Moillesulaz customs office, next to the stream that separates Geneva and France, a now rickety house was once a passing point for those fleeing the Nazi regime during the Second World War. This house sits astride the border: its entrance is in France, but its windows overlook a lawn in Switzerland.

From 1940 to 1944, its owner, Irène Gubier, helped a large number of Jews pass from one country to the other. They simply had to go through the house, then cross a field and finally the stream. Gubier owned another house in Aix-les-Bains, where she had housed a couple of Jews from the beginning of the war. For many long months, they directed their fellow Jews to this safe house… Alas, not all made it as the Genevan authorities sent back many of these refugees.

Irène Gubier, who was 43 years old in 1940, had lived this dangerous life since her adolescence, as the French secret service used her house to enter Switzerland without attracting attention. Her help to persecuted Jews lasted essentially from the summer of 1941 to the summer of 1942. Then, she became part of the Gilbert network and was put in charge of transmitting clandestine mail and helping diplomats to cross the border, which is why the house was called "The Ambassadors Passage". In fact, Colonel Groussard, alias Gilbert, directed this network from Geneva where he had taken refuge after fleeing the Vichy regime in France. Switzerland was a practical hub for meeting British agents or receiving aid from Swiss anti-Nazis. As a precaution, Irène Gubier thus had to stop helping individual refugees at the end of the summer of 1942.

As the plaque mounted on the façade indicates, Irène Gubier was finally arrested on 20 January 1944 and deported to the concentration camp for women in Ravensbrück, northern Germany.

DANS CETTE MAISON
IMPORTANT LIEU DE PASSAGE
S'ILLUSTRA DE 1940 A 1944
IRENE GUBIER Lieutenant
DES FORCES FRANCAISES COMBATTANTES
OFFICIER DE LA LEGION D'HONNEUR
ARRETEE LE 20 JANVIER 1944
ELLE FUT DEPORTEE
AU CAMP DE CONCENTRATION
DE RAVENSBRUCK

THREE HEROES AMONG MANY OTHERS

Father Louis Favre directed the Saint Francis Salesian School, the "Juvenat", at Ville-la-Grand. The large wall at the back of the property was on the border of the canton of Geneva. Using a ladder, 2,000 "clandestine" individuals – including several hundred Jewish children and adolescents – were able to pass over to the other side. Arrested and tortured by the Germans, Father Louis Favre was executed by firing squad on 16 July 1944.

Priest Marius Jolivet, the Parish priest of Collonges-sous-Salève, aided by his parishioners, helped hundreds of Jewish women, children and elderly people cross into Switzerland (there was a separate network for men). Of fragile health, he relentlessly pursued his activities as priest, rescuer and resistant, leaving himself no time to rest. He died in 1964.

Priest Jean Rosay, of Douvaine, organized a network that allowed hundreds of Jewish children and adolescents to cross the Swiss border. Arrested on 11 February 1944, he was deported to Auschwitz, then transferred to Birkenau, where he died one month before the camp's liberation.

THE LAST DOUBLE-DECKER BENCH

Rondeau de Chêne-Bougeries
• Bus 8, Conches stop

I t is possible to be both modest and historic. This double-decker bench, located at the Conches roundabout at Chêne-Bougeries, is a valuable testimony to the path taken every day by 18th-century Savoyard peasants as they went to sell their farm produce in the city of Geneva.

"This bench tells you of a now distant time..."

These women carried their baskets on their heads and, thanks to this ingenious double-decker bench, they didn't have to bend down. They simply slipped their load onto the upper plank, and then took a seat on the lower one.

A plaque bearing a text by Henri de Ziegler recalls this bench's unique role:

Stop here, traveller. This bench invites you to listen. It will tell you of a now distant time when farm women heading to market on foot from Savoy brought their eggs, vegetables and fruit to the city. They set their baskets above to take a short rest from their long journey. Do as they did and let yourself daydream in this charming spot. There were other benches similar to this one near Geneva. Today, this is the last. It is a rustic monument that reminds us of a time much less busy than ours. You will find it to be a pleasant memory.

For the better-off peasants who owned a donkey-cart, the nearby fishpond

(a small pond where freshwater fish were raised) provided a watering hole for the animals. This region, which was rather marshy at the time, consisted of empty fields and meagre pastures, called *bougeries*, which gave this village its name.

Wolves were also found here. In 1774, as the Savoyard soldiers had refused to give the peasants from Chêne weapons to hunt the beasts, they poisoned dogs and abandoned them in the forest to serve as bait!

THE MYSTERIOUS PAVILION
OF PONT-DE-SIERNE

⓫

2, route du Pas-de-l échelle
Veyrier
• Bus 8, Pont-de-Sierne stop

*The secret
hideaway
of Liszt's
mistresses?*

Countless rumours, now well forgotten, were once spread about this strange little house located just above the restaurant of Pont-de-Sierne and whose door is now walled up…

It seems that Franz Liszt secretly kept another of his mistresses here while he was staying in Geneva with Marie d'Agoult.

This pavilion must have been the perfect love nest. Built in the second half of the 19th century, it has three floors, each containing a single room. The façade originally held two plaster medallions, representing Orpheus on the left and Hercules on the right, but Hercules has recently disappeared. On the side wall, chubby-cheeked cherubs flutter about on bas-reliefs.

According to a few newspaper columnists, this abundant decoration, uncommon on such a doll's house, was supposedly saved from the demolition of Geneva's first theatre built in Bastions (1880-1881).

The pavilion also served as a set for Swiss native Jean-Louis Roy's movie *Black Out*, released in 1970, in which an old couple lock themselves into this tiny house with an enormous supply of food, convinced that the apocalypse of all-out war is near. They finally come out months later, having nearly gone mad. With their hands in the air, they wander along a road in the early morning, believing they are surrounded by "enemies"…

THE EXACT SITE
OF FERDINAND LASSALLE'S DUEL

12

Veyrier Forest
Chemin des Bûcherons
Bus 8, Stand-de-Veyrier stop

*A duel
at gunpoint
for the hand
of a beautiful
Hélène*

Today, few Genevans can locate the exact site of the duel at gunpoint in Veyrier forest on 28 August 1864 that led to the death of Ferdinand Lassalle. A large erratic stone block, along the chemin des Bûcherons – it was moved a few metres when a group of villas was built – marks the spot, however.

President of the first large Socialist party in Europe, the General German Workers' Association, Lassalle was a German Jew who Frenchified his name by adding an "le" ending to his original name, Lassal. The heart's desire of this man from a well-off family was a more just world, which led him to become involved in numerous social struggles.

Although a mature man, Ferdinand Lassalle was passionately in love with a blond, 20-year-old Bavarian girl, Hélène von Dönniges. She was engaged, however, to a student nearer her age from a noble Romanian family, Yanko de Racowitz. Hélène, despite her family's firm opposition, first responded to Ferdinand's mad love for her before starting to distance herself from him due to pressure, threats, and her own flighty character. Ferdinand Lassalle refused to accept the separation and sparked off a duel with Hélène's father (in charge of Teutonic affairs in Switzerland) by accusing him of keeping the happy couple apart. The father backed out of the duel, taking refuge in Bern. To save the family's honour, Hélène's young fiancé, Yanko, took up the gauntlet. Inexperienced, he stood up to Lassalle, a formidable marksman.

The duel took place in a clearing, near the Veyrier firing range. Yanko fired first, before the referee of the combat gave him the order, lodging a bullet in Lassalle's abdomen. Lassalle consequently missed his target…

Ferdinand Lassalle died three days later in a room at the Victoria Hotel, on 31 August, at the age of 40.

A modest stele was erected in his memory in 1891 in Bossey, near the Black Pond, by the Genevan chapter of the General German Workers' Association, and thus on the other side of the border, in France. They did so to respect the judicial practices of both countries, as duels to the death were not punished so severely as they were in Switzerland at the time. This monument now stands on the Bossey golf course – built in 1983 – near hole number 8 (photo opposite).

A disciple of Karl Marx, Ferdinand Lassalle, who wanted the State to become social through democratic routes, could have had a national destiny in Germany. Condemned for his political activities, he spent several months of his life in prison.

The beautiful Hélène de Racowitz – who later married her lover's murderer! – served as a model for Jean-Baptiste Carpeaux for his famous group sculpture *La Danse*, which graces the entrance to the Opéra Garnier in Paris. Her face was used for the central character, the *Génie* (spirit) of the dance, but the statue's body is that of a man, modelled on a carpenter named Sébastien Visat. This group sculpture caused quite a scandal at the time (1867). Today, the original is in the Orsay Museum in Paris; a copy by sculptor Paul Belmondo has replaced it on the opera house.

THE CATHOLIC CROSS OF SÉZENOVE

Village of Sézenove
• Bus L, towards Avusy-Village

> **A symbol of protest**

Erected at the behest of priest M. Merme (the inscription is marked on its white limestone base), the Catholic cross at the entrance to the village of Sézenove is unique in the canton of Geneva for the richness of the characters and floral symbols carved in its ironwork.

The symbolism of this cross, however, is more important than its originality or beauty. It stands for the protests of the Catholic communities against the Protestant powers.

In the early 19th century, the unification of twenty-four Catholic Savoyard villages, decided by the treaties of Turin of 1816, was the final touch to the absorption of eight other villages in 1815 (Treaty of Paris). At a time when

the Catholic populations were showing signs of rebellion (mainly from 1840 to 1870), crosses were erected near the main crossroads. They clearly indicated the religion of the "reunited" village.

These crosses were rarely placed in open country. The one at Signal de Bernex (the second highest spot in the canton, at 509m, after Moniaz, 516m) was the most famous exception (Mission 1850). This dominant position emphasized the strong Catholic following of the neighbouring villages, such as Bernex, Confignon, Laconnex or Onex.

According to the most recent statistics, the Genevan population is 39.5% Roman Catholic and 17.4% Protestant.

Right next to the Catholic cross is one of the most remarkable Genevan covered fountains. Its six basins arranged in two rows hold the cantonal records. Those carved in white stone date from 1822, while those in cement date from 1921.

THE JUSTICE STONE

• Bus L, Soral stop, then a 15-minute walk to La Feuillée

> ## *The Justice Stone has returned to Soral*

I n mid-September 2009, Soral's Justice Stone finally returned to Genevan soil. It had been moved in 1995 by four people from Norcier, a French village of the Saint-Julien-en-Genevois district. Their act was motivated by the desire to preserve a historic landmark from the traffic of trucks heading to and from the nearby gravel pit, rather than to steal it. Their concern was justified. Originally, there were two Justice Stones, but the construction of the Soral road in the 19th century led to the destruction of one of them. The surviving Justice Stone was thus placed on French territory, at the foot of a poplar tree where two paths crossed (photo below). A panel explained the history of this granite block that has four holes on one side, notches that were probably used to hold a wooden plank and an engraved cross.

The moving of the stone marked the beginning of a long quarrel, with the Soral authorities demanding that it be returned. The negotiations lasted fourteen years…

Today, the Justice Stone has been reinstalled at the place known as La Feuillée (photo opposite), alongside the Soral road, even if this is not its

exact initial position. Originally, it was located a few metres from stone marker 49, but this marker was moved when Switzerland and France exchanged plots of land and made changes to the border in 1966 during construction of the motorway.

WHAT IS THE JUSTICE STONE?

The Justice Stone marked the spot where prisoners were turned over to the lord of Ternier manor by the priests of Saint Victor priory. The priests, bound by canonical law, were forbidden to carry out violent punishments. It was thus the lord who held the "right of ultimate torment", according to the Seyssel agreements of 1124. Naked and chained, the prisoners condemned to death were thus given over to the soldiers and Ternier's executioner. Sometimes, the punishments were limited to simple mutilations, carried out at Norcier on the "ear-cutting stone".

BOUNDARY MARKERS

> *The boundary markers telling of Geneva's complex past*

Geneva has 105km of borders with France, but only 4.5km with the canton of Vaud and the rest of Switzerland. This position as an enclave explains the considerable number of boundary markers that mark its perimeter on the French side: 268 markers on the Haute-Savoie border, and 207 on the border with the Ain region.

The eventful history of these territories also brought its share of complications, which the markers illustrate: Sardinia and its eagle with its wings spread wide, France and its royal fleur-de-lis, Geneva with its eagle and key… These symbols are engraved in the stone and act as reminders of the successive treaties that shaped this region.

Over time, the border changes left traces that are sometimes picturesque.

The exchange of territory in 1963, when Geneva airport had to be enlarged and thus encroached on French territory, played a part in the scattering of markers that had become obsolete. There was no real administrative order to this scattering…

For example, marker 73 was mysteriously moved from Meyrin/Prévessin to a private property in Soral where it has become a decorative element, embedded in a wrought-iron gate! Of course, it no longer marks an official border.

Marker 1, at Chancy, is the westernmost point of the canton of Geneva, and thus of Switzerland. In 1993, this position earned it the honour of a visit from the offices of the Grand Councils of German Switzerland, Tessin and Geneva, accompanied by the French authorities. A plaque recalling this event

was affixed to an erratic stone block located 383 m from the marker, as surveyor Jean-Paul Wisard, the author of a rigorous official inventory of the Genevan markers, stated.

A few, sometimes comic, surprises should be noted. For example, near a hedge halfway between the customs office of Perly/St-Julien and the customs point on the roadside, stands marker 61 bearing an upside-down S for Sardinia! The mistake was probably caused by an illiterate stone carver who failed to position his *chablon** correctly for the engraving.

**chablon*: a Swiss-French term meaning "stencil"

ALPHABETICAL INDEX

ALPHABETICAL INDEX

THEMATIC INDEX

CURIOSITIES

HISTORY

THEMATIC INDEX

PEOPLE

RELIGION

SCULPTURES

Photo credits:

All photos were taken by **Christian Vellas** with the exception of:

Saint-Gervais Archaeological Site: Eric Aldag. Border markers: Jean-Paul Wisard.
Bossey golf course: Joël Vellas.
Credits for other illustrations: rue des Barrières, engraving by H.C. Forestier (1900). Muret building, Willy Aeschlimann collection. The prodigal son, detail of an Aubusson tapestry. Lions passage c. 1920, Gad-Borel Boissonnas collection. Inauguration of the national monument, Museum of Art and History, Vieux-Genève collection. Port de la Fusterie autrefois (Fusterie port in the past), engraving by L. Hess. Engraving of the Escalade by Franz Hogenberg (1603). Portraits: © DR.

Acknowledgements: Gad Borel-Boissonnas, Corinne Charles, Daniel Hameline, Armand Lombard, Flurin Spescha, Corinne Walker, Jean-Paul Wisard.

Cartography: **Jean-Baptiste Neny**
Design: **Roland Deloi**
Layout: **Stéphanie Benoit**
English translation: **Kimberly Bess**
Proof-reading: **Caroline Lawrence**

© JONGLEZ 2010
Registration of copyright: September 2010 – Edition: 01
ISBN: 978-2-9158-0780-6
Printed in France by Mame - 37000 Tours